IMAGES OF WAR

ON TO ROME

ANZIO & VICTORY AT CASSINO, 1944

RARE PHOTOGRAPHS FROM WARTIME ARCHIVES

Jon Diamond

Pen & Sword
MILITARY

First published in Great Britain in 2018 by
PEN & SWORD MILITARY
An imprint of
Pen & Sword Books Ltd
47 Church Street
Barnsley
South Yorkshire
S70 2AS

ISBN 978-1-52673-253-8

A CIP catalogue record for this book is available from the British Library.

Typeset by Concept, Huddersfield, West Yorkshire HD4 5JL.
Printed and bound in India by Replika Press Pvt. Ltd.

Pen & Sword Books Limited incorporates the imprints of Atlas, Archaeology, Aviation, Discovery, Family History, Fiction, History, Maritime, Military, Military Classics, Politics, Select, Transport, True Crime, Air World, Frontline Publishing, Leo Cooper, Remember When, Seaforth Publishing, The Praetorian Press, Wharncliffe Local History, Wharncliffe Transport, Wharncliffe True Crime and White Owl.

For a complete list of Pen & Sword titles please contact
PEN & SWORD BOOKS LIMITED
47 Church Street, Barnsley, South Yorkshire S70 2AS, England
E-mail: enquiries@pen-and-sword.co.uk
Website: www.pen-and-sword.co.uk

Contents

Acknowledgements

This archival photograph volume in the *Images of War* series is dedicated to the men and women who fought and perished in southern and central Italy during the early autumn of 1943 and extending well into 1944 to wrest control of the Italian mainland from the Nazis. We ponder upon viewing the photographs about the heroic sacrifice made to maintain freedom lest we forget. The author also wishes to acknowledge the many military history scholars, past and present, including such names as Blumenson, Graham, Bidwell, D'Este, Ellis, Neillands, Strawson, Konstam, Zaloga, Ford, Clark, Atkinson and Whitlock, to name but a few, who have catalogued the nuances of this protracted campaign with their superlative prose. The author is indebted to the able assistance of the archivists at both the United States Army Military History Institute (USAMHI) at the United States Army War College in Carlisle, Pennsylvania, and the Still Photo Section of the National Archives and Records Administration (NARA) in College Park, Maryland.

Chapter One

Strategic Prelude to the Campaign for Rome

Astalemate had developed along the Nazi defensive Gustav Line to the south of Rome during early February 1944, particularly at the town of Cassino, situated across the Rapido River, with the towering Benedictine abbey looming above overlooking the Liri Valley and the pathway to Rome. British prime minister Winston Churchill desperately wanted to capture the Eternal City, despite Italy's capitulation to become an Allied co-belligerent.

Before the battles for Rome, a series of see-saw campaigns (the Benghazi Handicap) pitted General Archibald Wavell's Western Desert Force (later to become, first, British XIII Corps and then Eighth Army under General Claude Auchinleck) and the Axis in the Cyrenaican third of Libya from December 1940 through to August 1942. Then, the British Eighth Army, under Lieutenant-General Bernard Montgomery, won the decisive Second Battle of El Alamein in November 1942 and commenced the pursuit of German Field-Marshal Erwin Rommel's German–Italian *PanzerArmee Afrika* across the Libyan Desert into south-eastern Tunisia. Coincident with this was Operation Torch, the Allied invasion of French north-west Africa near Casablanca, Oran and Algiers in Morocco and Algeria. After the rapid capitulation of Vichy French forces there, six months of bloody Tunisian combat ensued with the ultimate surrender of Axis bridgeheads in Bizerte and Tunis in early May 1943. With the Allied commander, General Dwight Eisenhower, having amassed a large expeditionary force in North Africa, along with Churchill's zeal to knock Italy out of the war and tie down German formations along Europe's soft underbelly, Sicily was invaded on 10 July 1943 during Operation Husky. The Allied Seventh and Eighth Armies, under the command of Lieutenant-General George Patton, and Montgomery, respectively, required thirty-eight days to force a tenacious Axis foe to evacuate the island to the Italian mainland across the Strait of Messina on 17 August. Benito Mussolini had been ousted in late July, and on 8 September the Italian government capitulated, precipitating a Nazi seizure of Italy. On 3 September Eighth Army's British XIII Corps staged the uncontested Operation Baytown and seized many locales along the Calabrian toe of Italy, while elements of the British 1st Airborne Division amphibiously landed at Taranto, Operation Slapstick, along the peninsula's heel on 9 September.

On 9 September, a larger Allied amphibious assault landed Lieutenant-General Mark Clark's Fifth Army's British X and US VI Corps along the Gulf of Salerno, to Naples' south. Initial attempts by only the German 16th Panzer Division failed to dislodge the Allies from their beachheads. However, within days, German Tenth Army commander General Heinrich von Vietinghoff amassed the XIV and LXXVI Panzer Corps and struck the Allied perimeter, almost compelling Clark's evacuation of the US VI Corps from the battlefield's southern end and re-situating it in British X Corps' northern sector. On 18 September, Vietinghoff withdrew his Nazi divisions to a temporary defensive line along the Volturno River, north of Naples. The Allies entered the Neapolitan port on 1 October and began extensive repair of the German-demolished dock facilities. German Field-Marshal Albert Kesselring, commanding the Nazi forces in southern Italy, ordered Vietinghoff to hold the Volturno River line until 15 October, enabling the completion of the more temporary Barbara and Bernhardt Lines, while more substantive fortifications were erected on the Gustav Line, which ran along the Garigliano and Rapido Rivers, stretching from the Tyrrhenian Sea in the west to north of the Sangro River's mouth on the Adriatic Sea coast in the east.

While Montgomery's Eighth Army units battled to the east of the Apennine Mountain spine at such locales as Fossacesia, Mozzogrogna, Orsogna and Ortona, Clark's Fifth Army campaigned in a wet, cold climate amid the massif comprising the

Strategic Situation: The First Battle for Cassino, late January 1944. The Allied Fifth and Eighth Armies reached the Gustav Line's defences after three months of mountain fighting and river crossings following the Salerno victory. British Eighth Army's XIII and V Corps' divisions were north of the Sangro and Moro Rivers after the gruesome battles for Orsogna and Ortona. The Adriatic sector became static south of the Rome Line. Along US Fifth Army's Tyrrhenian Sea coast sector, British X Corps assaulted the Garigliano River on 17 January with mixed results. The British 5th and 56th Divisions crossed and attacked Minturno and moved towards the foothills of the Aurunci Mountain, respectively, before the latter formation was repelled by the Nazi XIV Panzer Corps. The British 46th Division's crossing failed and had to be diverted into the 56th Division's area. From 20–22 January, US II Corps attempted an entrance to the Liri Valley with a Rapido River assault by the 141st and 143rd Infantry Regiments of the US 36th Division, which ended in disaster. The 36th Division's uninvolved 142nd Regiment was attached to the US 34th Infantry Division, and these four II Corps regiments successfully crossed the Rapido to Cassino's north. Amid logistically challenged combat in the Monte Cairo massif, these American units almost succeeded in outflanking the Nazi defences at Cassino, advancing to within 1,000 yards of the Benedictine abbey, where they remained until Eighth Army's 4th Indian Division relieved them on 12 February. The French Expeditionary Corps' (FEC) Moroccan 2nd and Algerian 3rd Divisions crossed the Rapido River to the north of the US 34th Division on 24 January. The FEC, demonstrating their mountain fighting abilities, captured some heights in the Monte Cairo massif south of Atina. The exhausted and combat-depleted Fifth Army's II Corps now needed Leese's Eighth Army divisions to cross the Apennines to assist with the stalled Gustav Line offensive. On 22 January, Fifth Army's VI Corps amphibiously assaulted Anzio. Days of beachhead consolidation rather than a move towards Rome enabled the Nazis to contain the invasion. The Allies now had two separate fronts to combat Kesselring's interior lines and formidable defences. (Philip Schwartzberg, Meridian Mapping, Minneapolis, MN)

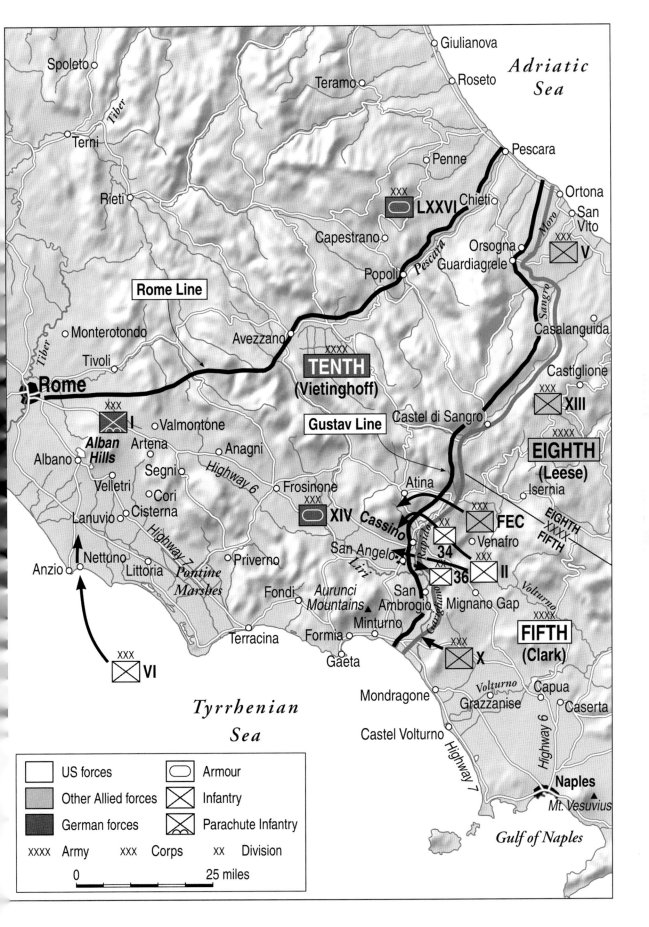

pillars of the Mignano Gap, in an attempt to gain entry into the Liri Valley to the south of Cassino and then on to Rome. After Clark's disastrous attempt to cross the Rapido River in front of Cassino with his US 36th Division ended in failure on 20–22 January 1944, his II Corps' reinforced US 34th Division, along with the French Expeditionary Corps (FEC), the latter under the capable French general Alphonse Juin, almost seized the Benedictine abbey and Monte Cassino during the early days of February. However, their attacks faltered amid a determined Nazi resistance and Allied exhaustion, as the II New Zealand Corps was held in reserve rather than committed to the tail-end of the hard-pressed Allied mountain attack north of the town. The First Battle of Cassino ended with the Germans in possession of the town, the heights and the monastery looming above.

(**Opposite**) The British Army's architects of Operation Compass: Lieutenant-General Richard O'Connor, commander Western Desert Force (*left*) and General Archibald Wavell, commander-in-chief, Middle East Command (*right*) review plans for their 'five-day raid', which employed the 4th Indian Division and the British 7th Armoured Division against the Italian Tenth Army's fortified camps and garrison at Sidi Barrani that commenced on 9 December 1940. The Australian 6th Division replaced the Indian infantry and captured Bardia on 5 January 1941 and, then, drove on towards Tobruk. (*Author's Collection*)

(**Above**) A British Crusader tank climbs over an anti-tank ditch as it moves forward in support of Eighth Army infantry at the start of Operation Crusader on 18 November 1941 to relieve Tobruk. German General Rommel, commander of the *Deutsche Afrika Korps* (DAK) arrived in Tripoli on 12 February 1941, but quickly attacked eastward, seizing ground gained by O'Connor's offensive and investing Tobruk by April. Tobruk's siege was lifted on 10 December after an epic eight-month siege. (*NARA*)

(**Above**) General Claude Auchinleck, now the acting general officer commanding (GOC), Eighth Army, after the disastrous Gazala battles of May–June 1942 and the Axis capture of Tobruk on 21 June, discusses the retreat of his British 50th Division along the Via Balbia to incomplete lines during the final week of June, first at Mersa Matruh and then at El Alamein, with Rommel's *PanzerArmee Afrika* 'on his heels'. (*Library of Congress*)

(**Opposite, above**) An Eighth Army Vickers machine-gun crew watch a bomb from a *Luftwaffe Stuka* dive-bomber explode in the open Western Desert between Mersa Matruh and El Alamein. This was the scene of Auchinleck's First Battle of El Alamein, a series of indecisive engagements in July, which did halt Rommel's drive on to Alexandria. (*NARA*)

(**Opposite, below**) An Eighth Army armoured column, led by a Crusader tank and followed by two M3 medium (Grant) tanks, enter Mersa Matruh after Montgomery's victorious offensive against Field-Marshal Rommel's *Panzer-Armee Afrika*. The Second Battle of El Alamein commenced on 23 October 1942 and ended on 4 November, as the Axis forces retreated for the Egyptian border along the coast road with Eighth Army in a cautious pursuit. (*NARA*)

(**Opposite, above**) Two British soldiers observe an American truck tow a small-calibre artillery piece from a British-crewed Landing Craft Mechanised (LCM) at the Les Andalouses landing beaches on 8 November 1942. This was part of the US 1st Infantry Division's amphibious assault task to capture the Algerian port of Oran on Operation Torch's D-Day. (*NARA*)

(**Above**) The crew of a US 1st Infantry Division 33rd Field Artillery Battalion's 105mm M2A1 Howitzer fire a shell to support an American counter-offensive at Kasserine Pass in late February 1943 after the previous stinging defeat there. An Arab mud-brick house was utilised for concealment. (*NARA*)

(**Opposite, below**) Elements of the Eighth Army's Gordon Highlanders are led by a piper across the Libyan border into south-eastern Tunisia in February 1943. Montgomery's supply chain was extremely lengthy after crossing both the Egyptian frontier and all of Libya, and it was to take weeks before Eighth Army concentrated to attack the Mareth Line on 20 March. (*NARA*)

(**Opposite, above**) British infantrymen of the 7th Rifle Brigade from X Corps' 7th Motor Brigade defend a position consisting of a recently captured chest-high stone wall in the Kounine hills during Eighth Army's advance toward Tunis in April 1943. (*USAMHI*)

(**Above**) Two Eighth Army infantrymen stare into the Mediterranean Sea from the farthest point north on the Cape Bon peninsula in Tunisia after the massive Axis surrender in Tunis and Bizerte in early May 1943. General Harold Alexander fulfilled the Allied mission to clear North Africa of all Axis troops. After much planning and military deception, the Italian island of Sicily was to be invaded to carry the Allied campaign from the African continent to southern Europe. (*NARA*)

(**Opposite, below**) A British Universal Carrier and a towed gun land on an Eighth Army beach along Sicily's eastern coast on 10 July 1943 as Landing Ship Tanks (LSTs) and Landing Craft Infantry (LCIs) unload vehicles and infantrymen (*background*). Other ingeniously designed shallow draft vessels, such as Landing Craft Tanks (LCTs), Landing Craft Vehicle/Personnel (LCVP), and Landing Craft Mechanised (LCM), solved the centuries-old problem of moving troops rapidly from ship to shore. (*Author's Collection*)

(**Opposite, above**) Infantrymen from the 1st Canadian Division in their combat debut move off their Bark West landing zone. A shack (*left*) that housed an Italian machine-gun position was captured by Royal Marine (RM) Commandos in a hand-grenade attack moments earlier to assist the Canadians' inland movement. The RM Commandos landed prior to the Canadians west of the Ponte Castellazo on the Pachino peninsula to anchor the extreme left flank of Eighth Army's assault. (*NARA*)

(**Opposite, below**) A destroyed Italian armoured vehicle of Mobile Group E, which actually was a captured French Renault R-35 infantry tank, in the town of Gela. On 10 July 1943, elements of Colonel William Darby's 1st and 4th Ranger Battalions (Force X) and some US Combat Engineers encountered and defeated advancing units of this Italian armoured formation utilising bazookas and a 37mm anti-tank gun, enabling Gela's seizure. (*NARA*)

(**Above**) An American 155mm 'Long Tom' cannon is towed by a prime mover near Troina in Sicily's central mountainous region. The US 1st and elements of the 9th Infantry Divisions required five days to seize this mountaintop locale in their eastward drive to capture Randazzo and a road network to Messina. The combat ordeal was a harbinger of the upcoming mountainous warfare on the Italian mainland. (*NARA*)

(**Opposite, above**) On 5 August 1943, British XIII Corps infantrymen moved in single-file, alert for enemy snipers, amid Catania's ruins, an eastern Sicilian port and major objective of Montgomery's Eighth Army on the road to Messina. The heavily bombarded city fell to the British after the withdrawal of the Nazi Hermann Göring Division. (*NARA*)

(**Opposite, below**) American infantrymen from the US 3rd Division patrol a major street in Messina past the Bank of Sicily on 17 August 1943. The Axis evacuation across the Strait of Messina to the Italian mainland completed that day. (*NARA*)

(**Above**) Canadian infantrymen lead their supply-laden donkey along a narrow hillside path inland from their uncontested landing at Reggio during Operation Baytown's invasion of the Italy's Calabrian toe. Inadequate roads, motor transport shortage, and the delaying tactical withdrawal of the Nazi LXXVI Panzer Corps slowed Montgomery's advance north towards the Salerno battlefield. (*NARA*)

(**Opposite, above**) An American M7 Gun Motor Carriage or self-propelled gun (SPG) vehicle, which housed a 105mm Howitzer upon a M3 medium tank chassis fires rounds at enemy armour. The British Army dubbed this armoured vehicle the 'Priest', due to its pulpit-like machine-gun in the front. Allied armoured SPGs were vital in breaking up German 16th Panzer Division's attacks, which almost reached US VI Corps' shoreline positions on 9 September 1943. (*NARA*)

(**Opposite, below**) British infantrymen from the 6th Queens Regiment of the British 56th Division's 169th Brigade run past a pair of destroyed Panzer IV tanks on an inland road through the hills overlooking the Salerno beachhead after Nazi resistance and fierce armoured counter-attacks failed to dislodge the Allied X and VI Corps from their perimeter. On 18–19 September 1943, German Tenth Army commander von Vietinghoff began to withdraw his formations towards the Volturno River defences north of Naples. (*NARA*)

(**Above**) A Universal Carrier of the Guards Brigade of the British 56th Division enters Battipaglia's ruins on 18 September 1943. On 10 September, the 9th Battalion Royal Fusiliers, after having entered Battipaglia, was counter-attacked by strong elements of the German 16th Panzer Division. Some in the British infantry battalion retreated from this railway town while others surrendered. For the ensuing week, heavy fighting raged along the banks of the Tusciano River before the British re-entered Battipaglia. (*NARA*)

(**Opposite, above**) After the Allied battles for the Salerno beachhead had been won along with units' consolidation and reinforcements, the advance northwards to Naples and beyond to the Volturno River occurred. Here, US infantrymen search Italian buildings for enemy stragglers and snipers, which delayed the Allied advance. (*NARA*)

(**Opposite, below**) A platoon from the 10th Royal Berkshire Regiment of the 168th Brigade of British X Corps' 56th Division scale some of the steep rocky hills of Calvi Risorta north of Teano in November 1943. The heights in the background and the hastily erected defences of the Bernhardt Line were to be formidable obstacles. The Bernhardt Line was a defensive belt lying north of the Barbara Line and south of the Gustav Line. All three fortification belts comprised the German Winter Line defences that spanned the waist of the Italian peninsula. (*NARA*)

(**Above**) British infantrymen of the 1st London Scottish Regiment of the 56th Division's 168th Brigade scale a stone wall during their attack on Monastery Hill (Point 963) in the Monte Camino massif sector of the Bernhardt Line in December 1943. In early November, this same unit failed to evict Nazi 15th Panzer Grenadier Division defenders from the height, necessitating a pause in the combat for two weeks. Monte Camino, which formed a shoulder of the Mignano Gap 16 miles to the south-east of Cassino, had to be taken for the Allied Fifth Army's assault on Cassino and then Rome via the Liri Valley. After several attempts, the British were able to seize and hold the summit of Monte Camino by 6 December. (*USAMHI*)

(**Opposite, above**) A US 34th Infantry Division lieutenant spots enemy activity on Monte Trocchio from Monte La Chiaia in mid-January 1944. Both of these lesser heights were situated in the valley between the Mignano Gap's Monte Camino–Monte la Difensa–Monte Lungo massif to the south and Montes Cassino and Cairo as well as the Rapido River to the north. The US 2nd Corps captured Monte Trocchio on 15 January in order to secure a start line for the US 36th Division's disastrous Rapido River assault a week later. (*USAMHI*)

(**Above**) In the Eighth Army sector in October 1943, a patrol of the Canadian 1st Infantry Division ascends steep hills above Bojano near Campobasso. Italian mountain towns (*background*) had narrow streets and bunched buildings, ideal for Nazi snipers. The Canadians became expert house-to-house combatants. (*NARA*)

(**Opposite, below**) Along a narrow residential street of the Adriatic port-city of Ortona, a Canadian 6-pounder anti-tank gun crew is seen pushing their weapon towards a firing position against a fortified Nazi bunker containing machine-guns and *panzerfausts* amid the rubble. (*NARA*)

(**Opposite, above**) Mortarmen of the US 36th Infantry Division fire their 81mm weapon to support the Rapido River assault on 20–22 January 1944. Intentionally flooded to become 25–50 feet wide and 9 feet deep, fording the river was impossible and, during daylight, bridging equipment and assault boats were shelled under direct observation from Monte Cassino. During either daylight crossings with concealing smokescreens or after dark, the 36th Division's two attacking regiments suffered grievously. (*USAMHI*)

(**Above**) North African *Goumiers* of General Alphonse Juin's French Expeditionary Corps man their American .30-inch calibre Browning light machine-gun amid the rubble of an Italian village across the Rapido River north of both the town of Cassino and the Benedictine abbey atop Monte Cassino. The Algerian and Moroccan troops were successful in capturing some Nazi-held positions south of Atina at January 1944's end. (*NARA*)

(**Opposite, below**) The crew of an American 57mm anti-tank gun readies for an anticipated German counter-attack after the failed US 36th Infantry Division's Rapido River assault on 20–22 January 1944. The snow-capped Monte Cairo (*far background*) towers over Monte Cassino below with its Benedictine abbey situated upon it. (*NARA*)

(**Above**) American infantrymen of the 34th Infantry Division positioned in their fortified slit trench across the Rapido after elements from this unit came within 1,000 yards of the monastery atop Monte Cassino during the First Battle for Cassino from 24 January–11 February 1944. (*NARA*)

(**Opposite, above**) An American 105mm Howitzer manned by a Lebanese crew of the French Expeditionary Corps fires at German positions across the Rapido River north of Cassino in support of the attacks by the 2nd Moroccan and 3rd Algerian Divisions in late January 1944 during the First Battle for Cassino. (*NARA*)

(**Opposite, below**) The town of Cassino (*foreground*), Castle Hill beyond it (*middle*), and the Benedictine abbey upon Monte Cassino (*background*) on 6 February 1944, were the first two locales under Allied artillery-fire. The abbey remained untouched. However, it was bombarded into ruins during a controversial, massive Allied heavy and medium bomber air-raid as a prelude to the Second Battle for Cassino on 15 February. (*NARA*)

Chapter Two

Terrain, Fortifications and Weapons

During the combat to break through the Gustav Line and move through the Liri Valley on to Rome, Allied and German commanders and combatants were challenged by the 750-mile-long by 150-mile-wide Italian peninsula's formidable terrain, its crippling weather conditions, and the strategic dilemma of having to switch military resources to other war fronts and upcoming campaigns elsewhere.

The high, rugged peaks of the Apennine Mountains, which form a spine running down the peninsula, creates three zones: the eastern and western coastal plains and a central mountain region. This latter area, with its desolate, wilderness terrain, restricted combat to largely the two coastal flanks. Other massifs and flat-topped ridges extend in a parallel fashion to the coastal plains to form ribs emanating from the central Apennine spine. These ribs are separated from one another by tortuous river valleys that created separate tactical topographic blocks that hindered the Allied advance in Italy and nullified their armoured superiority and its self-propelled artillery (SPA).

For any advance, emphasis was placed on the Allied infantrymen's skills and endurance to fight this slog and the quartermasters' rudimentary means of sure-footed pack animals, manhandling and the occasional Jeep to provide the campaigns' supplies. These topographic blocks were ideal terrain features for the Nazi defenders, who in small numbers and with properly placed demolitions could channel the Allied advance into deadly fire-zones. Solid masonry mountain villages provided excellent observation points and cover for the Germans. Roads that crossed numerous flooded streams and narrow defiles in the winter of 1943–44 were also heavily mined and/or demolished by the Nazis.

Two geographic areas were the most suitable from a terrain standpoint for an Allied advance on to Rome. First, the Liri Valley's immediate vicinity was guarded by both Monte Cassino, situated in front of the towering 5,000-foot Monte Cairo massif to the north of the valley, and Monte Maio, located to the south of the valley, which rises to 3,000 feet projecting spurs into the valley south of the Liri River. Kesselring's forces had closed the entrance into the Liri Valley, which lies at the junction of the Liri,

Rapido and Garigliano Rivers, with the construction of the Gustav Line (see below). Second, the western coastal plain could be assaulted utilising the Allied overwhelming sea power to turn an enemy flank along the Tyrrhenian Sea coast. This coastal plain extends 100 miles to the north-west from the mouth of the Garigliano River to San Severo, 20 miles to Rome's west. Two topographic features limited Allied armoured thrusts here: the Alban Hills north of Anzio and the Pontine Marshes to that harbour's south-east. However, south of the Pontine Marshes, the coastal plain would be more favourable terrain for the deployment of armoured vehicles. The Allies at the start of 1944 were going to combat the German defenders at both locales: the Gustav Line at Monte Cassino and on the Tyrrhenian Sea coast at Anzio.

The Germans had other natural terrain advantages elsewhere while defending the Liri Valley. To the south, the valley was flanked by steep mountains that bordered the western side of the Garigliano all the way from the sea to the Liri River's bend. To the east, the mountain range widened north from Monte Sammucro to the Apennines, protecting the approach to the Liri Valley from the north via the Rapido River Valley. This range was dominated by peaks nearing 4,000 feet, was poorly inhabited, and almost devoid of natural routes of communication for advance of an army. Only two tortuous and narrow roads traversed this desolate landscape dominated by hilly peaks. The first one ran to Sant' Elia Flumerapido, north of Cassino, while the second coursed from where the Rapido made a north-eastward bend to a mountainous area between Colle Belvedere and Monte Cifalco and then north-westward to Atina.

The swiftly flowing Rapido River, 25–50 feet wide with steep banks, wound tortuously from its mountainous origin north of Monte Cassino and weaved in a southerly direction in front of Cassino, which was to become one of the most fortified towns during the Italian Campaign. The Germans diverted the river upstream from the assault area, making the approaches a sea of mud. The high ground on the far bank of the Rapido River, of which Monte Cassino formed part, comprised a series of heights. From the heights of Monte Cassino, the Germans observed and delivered fire on the entire area below, including the river's crossing site at Sant' Angelo. Some 2 miles to the west, Monte Cairo overlooked the lower heights from its peak over 5,000 feet high with the remaining heights ranging between 1,500 and 3,000 feet. As a final hurdle, troops that attempted to debouch into the Rapido Valley found themselves facing two isolated hills: Montes Trocchio and Porchia at 1,400 and 800 feet respectively. Both of these isolated hills were directly on the approach to Cassino and flanked the plain leading across the Rapido River into the Liri Valley. The US 36th Infantry Division's late-January 1944 attack across the Rapido River was doomed to fail as long as Monte Cassino, along with the hill country to the north and west, was possessed by the Nazis. In these mountainous defensive positions, the Germans positioned artillery and mortar regiments to rain fire on the entire offensive area of the 36th Division and large parts of the rear area of US II Corps.

Several miles downstream, the Rapido flowed into the Liri River near Sant' Ambroglio and then the confluence of both waterways became the Garigliano River, which then flowed south-west for 15 miles to the sea. The Rapido–Garigliano flood-plain and the steep uplands beyond it constituted the western end of the Gustav Line. Another 5-mile-wide floodplain was situated near the Garigliano River's mouth on the eastern side of the waterway, which made it hazardous to attack across this area.

After the Fifth Army's failure at the Rapido River on 20–22 January 1944, and with the exhausting but still unsuccessful attacks of the US 34th Infantry Division and the FEC north of Cassino, the Allied front stretched from the Gulf of Gaeta on the Tyrrhenian Sea coast north-eastward to the Adriatic. General Alexander, the Allied 15th Army Group commander, still believed that Cassino was the key to the gateway leading into the Liri Valley. However, he had to revise his strategy and tactics for a breakthrough. On the other hand, the Nazi commander, Field Marsh Kesselring, hoped the Allies would attack the Gustav Line at Monte Cassino and 'break their teeth' on it.

The Todt labour units of German service troops and impressed Italian civilians constructed an interlocking web of fortifications and obstacles. There were three of these main defensive battle-lines north and south of Rome. They were referred to as the Gustav, Hitler (also called Senger, Dora or Orange) and Gothic Lines, the latter running from Pisa to Rimini.

The Gustav Line crossed the Italian peninsula at its narrowest point, roughly 100 miles from the mouth of the Garigliano River on the Tyrrhenian Sea coast to the Adriatic Sea coast, just 2 miles north-west of Ortona, and incorporated some of the best defensive terrain features available. The most heavily defended portion of this defensive belt was anchored on the 5,000-foot Monte Cairo as the Liri Valley's northern shoulder and ran south-east to 1,700-foot Monte Cassino and along the western banks of the Rapido and Gari Rivers across the entrance to the valley. The Gari River began just south of Cassino town and met the Rapido River near Sant' Angelo. The Rapido River's swift-flowing current and steep banks made it a formid-able natural obstacle, which Kesselring supplemented with interlocking minefields, machine-gun pillboxes, concrete and steel entrenchments for field ordnance, barbed wire and rifle pits. This portion of the Gustav Line ended on the southern slopes of Monte Maio and then continued south of the village of Castelforte along high ground north of Minturno to the Tyrrhenian Sea.

Monte Cassino was the centrepiece of the Gustav Line with its defences in and around the town of Cassino, situated on the banks of the Rapido River, and in the immediate vicinity of the sixth-century Benedictine abbey above on the height prior to its destruction on 15 February 1944. The Nazi defence of this sector denied a swift

Allied entry into the Liri Valley and on to Rome from late January to mid-May 1944, which encompassed the failed First, Second and Third Battles for Cassino. Kesselring realised that the Gustav Line could not contain the Fifth and Eighth Armies south of Rome indefinitely. However, he reasoned that a delay to an Allied breakthrough there would forestall the strategically more important crossing of the northern Apennines into the Po Valley, which constituted the industrial and agricultural centres of Italy.

Around 5 to 10 miles beyond the Gustav Line in the Liri Valley was the Hitler Line. While the Hitler Line was not fixed on a natural obstacle, it too used terrain as a force-multiplier and it bristled with fieldworks making it formidable. Reliance on these defensive lines was vital for Kesselring as a manpower shortage was a huge Nazi handicap. Starting at Terracina, on the Tyrrhenian Sea coast north-west of the Garigliano River, the Hitler Line crossed the mountains near Pico and then continued into the Liri Valley through Pontecorvo. Rising slightly, the Hitler Line coursed into the Monte Cairo massif's southern slope at Aquino and then terminated at Piedimonte San Germano, a fortified village that loomed over the Liri Valley's floor, serving as an anchor as it covered the axis from Aquino to Pontecorvo. This latter locale was previously a rear echelon assembly area for Nazi troops to be fed into the Rapido River's battles via a series of local farm tracks to Pignataro.

The approaches to the Hitler Line's defences were covered with aprons of barbed wire and minefields, the latter sown along anticipated Allied armour movement paths. The spring months' tall grain and grass provided some natural cover for the attackers from the murderous sighted Nazi fields of fire. However, it precluded accurate Allied aerial detection of the minefields and camouflaged defensive works. These were visible only to advancing Allied infantry and armour as the gun ports typically were no higher than 3 feet above the ground. The hardened defences of the Hitler Line consisted of underground bunkers to protect the troops from aerial and artillery bombardment, rows of bottle-shaped machine-gun emplacements. Interspersed among these fortifications were dug-in turrets of Mk V (Panther) Panzers, *Panzerturm*, with their long 75mm AT gun capable of destroying any of the Allied tanks deployed against them. These were painted to blend in with the surrounding vegetation. Between the *Panzerturm* were trenches and emplacements for infantry and machine-guns, from which to launch local counter-attacks, and mobile AT guns concealed by wire camouflage nets with dried grass to obscure the positions' entry points while the depressed 75mm AT gun barrel depressed between rows of sandbags made such field fortifications invisible. Tactically, the Nazi defenders knew that Allied armour had to be destroyed to stop accompanying infantry advances.

The Melfa River was situated 5 miles west of the Hitler Line. The waterway drained out of the northern mountains and wound across the entire Liri Valley to a perpendicular junction with the Liri River. Behind its western bank, the Germans formed another defensive line. This too was to be an attack site for I Canadian Corps during the last days of May 1944.

Anzio was a small fishing village of 7,000 Italians, and Nettuno of similar size a mile away on the coast. The harbour at Anzio was small, but good for off-loading with a protective mole from the surf. To Anzio's north, there were sandy beaches and dunes, which were deemed quite suitable for the amphibious landing of troops and vehicles. The Moletta River, ran 10 miles north of Anzio, and was a northern demarcation point for the British sector. The upper reaches of the Moletta River were fed by deep gullies, which were to become the scenes of some future horrific combat. Allied aerial reconnaissance missed identifying several of these gullies, which were to impair British armoured movement. The Alban Hills, 3,000 feet high and 20 miles inland, were located to the north-east of the beachhead.

To the north of Anzio and Nettuno was the Mussolini Canal, 36 feet wide with its eastern branch bordering on the Pontine Marshes. This canal was to become an effective boundary as well as a defence line against enemy tank attack in the American sector. Just inland from Anzio were the Padiglione Woods. Beyond the woods was open pasture with a scattering of Italian farms.

There were three major Italian highways (Highways 5, 6 and 7) that led to Rome. Highway 5 was to the east of the Apennine on the Adriatic Sea coast, therefore farthest from the Eternal City. Highway 7 (the Appian Way) was on a narrow Tyrrhenian Sea coastal strip that Kesselring contested. Finally, Highway 6 through the Liri Valley offered the best route to Rome as it traversed through a natural breach in the mountains to the west of the Apennine spine.

There were two main roads in the Anzio perimeter apart from the coastal ones. First, the Via Anziate was a main thoroughfare from Anzio to Albano, paralleling the railroad past the station at Campoleone. The second main road began just to the north of the Pontine Marshes and led to Cisterna, 16 miles from Anzio and situated on Highway 7. Both roads were to be registered by Nazi artillery, limiting Allied movements. Highway 6, which ran through the Liri Valley past Cassino, was situated to the north of the Alban Hills. Highways 6 and 7 were the only two German supply routes to Cassino. Between Albano and Cisterna was the Italian town of Velletri, from which emanated a connecting road that skirted along the southern face of the Alban Hills to Highway 6 at Valmontone.

The Caesar Line was situated 50 miles to the west of the Hitler Line and just to the north of Valmontone situated on Highway 6. It was an undeveloped position behind the Hitler Line and constituted the last major German defensive position south of Rome. Early in April 1944, the Germans had hastily begun building this secondary defence line between the Anzio beachhead and Rome, utilising 10,000 Italian laborers under the direction of *Wehrmacht* engineers. The Caesar Line extended from the Tyrrhenian Sea north of Anzio across the southern flanks of the Alban Hills by Velletri and then north-eastward past Artena to Highway 6 near Valmontone. From there the defences extended over the Ernici Mountains to Sora on the road to Avezzano. The Caesar Line was only suitable for a delaying action as it lacked the heavy fortifications of the Hitler Line and did not possess the favourable terrain conditions of the Gustav Line.

Artillery support for infantry was, indeed, problematic for both combatant sides. The Italian mountaintops were situated between the targets and the trajectory of artillery gunfire created both accuracy and friendly fire pitfalls for the gunners. In order to overcome this terrain limitation, artillerymen resorted to plunging fire. However, to accomplish this, customary field pieces would have to be visible to the defenders and their counter-battery fire. As Allied intelligence had estimated that there were about 400 enemy ordnance pieces and rocket launchers located north of Highway 6 with about 150–200 of these able to fire in support of the defenders of Cassino town and Monte Cassino, Fifth and Eighth Armies' medium and heavy Allied artillery regiments had to be protectively situated behind Italian massifs such as Monte Trocchio to direct fire on targets such as Cassino and beyond. Despite this attempt at concealment, the Germans were still able to gauge the Allied artillery positions and mount effective counter-battery fire missions.

Mortars of all sizes, such as the British 3-inch and American 81mm types used at the infantry battalion level, provided plunging fire against narrow mountain ridges and reverse slopes. However, their range was still limited necessitating the presence of these weapons up close to the frontlines. Such a tactical concern for the mortarmen required that the weapons and the rounds had to be man- or mule-carried up into the mountains as roads were limited and trucks made inviting targets for the Nazi gunners perched on the heights above the valley below.

(**Opposite**) A US Twelfth Air Force B-26 twin-engined medium bomber releases its payload on bridges near Ceprano, halfway between Rome and Naples, to disrupt Nazi troop movements encircling the Anzio beachhead in late January 1944. Anti-aircraft flak bursts are located above. (*USAMHI*)

(**Above**) 'The Factory' at Aprilia (*foreground*) from the air north of Anzio Harbour. Although a fascist farming community, Aprilia was dubbed The Factory because of its prominent bell tower that resembled a smokestack. The Anzio battlefield was generally flat with little vegetation. Aprilia was located near the Via Anziate (*left*), which ran from Anzio to Albano. The Alban Hills (*background*) are off in the distance. (*USAMHI*)

(**Opposite, above**) The ruined village of Isola Bella in an aerial view just off the road that led to Cisterna (*background*) and the Alban Hills in the far distance. Infantry regiments of the US 3rd Division were to combat counter-attacking elements of both the Hermann Göring and 26th Panzer Divisions in this area. (*USAMHI*)

(**Opposite, below**) An aerial view of the Cassino battlefield with Monte Trocchio (*centre*) and the town of Cassino in the valley region just beyond with Castle Hill situated immediately above it. The Benedictine abbey atop Monte Cassino is to the left of the town and below the snowcapped Monte Cairo (*background*). The Rapido River is off to the right. (*NARA*)

(**Above**) Cassino town with Castle Hill above it on 24 February 1944. The area in front of the town had been flooded by the Germans to prevent an Allied armoured attack. (*USAMHI*)

(**Opposite, above**) An American M4 medium tank lies disabled in an area flooded by waters of the Rapido River that the Nazis had diverted to disrupt Allied mechanised advances on to the town of Cassino with Monte Cairo in left background. (*USAMHI*)

(**Opposite, below**) A patrol of the 143rd Infantry Regiment of US 36th Division is shown as it manoeuvres through some cultivated fields near Velletri on the Anzio Front in late May 1944. Velletri was located in the foothills of the Alban Hills between Albano to the west and Cori to the east. (*USAMHI*)

(**Above**) A British infantry section from the King's Shropshire Light Infantry Regiment eat rations under cover of an irrigation ditch before an advance at Anzio. The Anzio–Nettuno beachhead was situated on a coastal plain with the Pontine Marshes to the south-east. Numerous irrigation gullies, called *fossi*, were constructed before the war to drain the wetlands for malaria control and to promote farming. Bitter often hand-to-hand combat to possess these gullies were commonplace in both the American and British sectors. (*NARA*)

(**Opposite, above**) An M10 3-inch Gun Motor Carriage from a Tank Destroyer unit camouflaged behind a haystack on an Anzio farm within the perimeter's open terrain. The 0.50-inch calibre Browning machine-gunner at the rear of the open turret is readied for a low-level *Luftwaffe* attack. A forward crewman in the turret is shown looking for enemy movements out from the surrounding Alban Hills. (*USAMHI*)

(**Opposite, below**) Paratroopers from the 2nd Battalion of the US 504th Parachute Infantry Regiment cross the Mussolini Canal, the easternmost boundary of the Allied perimeter at Anzio. On 30 January, US Rangers met with calamity as their battalions were struck by Germans along the Fossi di Pantana irrigation ditch, an extension of the Mussolini Canal during their offensive on Cisterna. Of the 767 Rangers from the 1st and 3rd Battalions sent to Cisterna, only six returned. Approximately 450 Rangers surrendered while the rest were killed in action. (*USAMHI*)

(**Above**) British 1st Division infantrymen advance past a signpost for Rome along the Via Anziate shortly after landing during the last week of January 1944. As the British advanced northwards on Campoleone, units of this division created a salient, 'the Thumb', as German resistance stiffened, which was to become a site of fierce Nazi counter-attacks during February. (*NARA*)

(**Above**) A mortar platoon from a US 3rd Division infantry regiment moves up a dirt road from their beachhead perimeter towards Cisterna on Highway 7. Major counter-attacks from Cisterna by the Hermann Goring and 26th Panzer Divisions in early February compelled the 15th and 30th US Infantry Regiments to form a perimeter just to the north of Isola Bella. (*NARA*)

(**Opposite, above**) A British-crewed M4 medium tank on a dirt road near the Cassino battlefield passing entrenched British infantrymen at the roadside. The Eighth Army's XIII Corps had been shifted by Lieutenant-General Leese across the Apennines from the static Adriatic sector into the Cassino cauldron in early February 1944. (*NARA*)

(**Opposite, below**) A panoramic view of the Anzio–Nettuno beachhead on Operation Shingle's D-Day, 22 January 1944. Amphibious DUKWs are bringing supplies from the transports across bulldozed dunes covered with wire matting for traction towards inland supply dumps. (*USAMHI*)

American combat engineers span a ravine in the Cassino sector, which was demolished by the retreating Germans, with a temporary Bailey bridge. These 10-foot prefabricated steel truss bridge sections, named for the British War Office creator Donald Bailey, were transported to crossings for rapid assembly with simple tools. After the newly erected structure was pushed out across the span, a wood-planking road surface was added, capable of supporting a minimum of 20 tons. The Allies projected a need for 1,000 Bailey bridges to cover the Italian peninsula to the Po River. However, 3,000 Bailey bridges were erected in less than two years for a total distance of roughly 60 miles. (*USAMHI*)

Amid the ruins of the town of Cassino, an Eighth Army infantryman fires his Thompson 0.45-inch calibre submachine-gun against enemy positions while another is shown spotting behind him. (*NARA*)

A ruined portal of Cassino's Hotel Continental served as a German 88mm self-propelled gun (SPG) redoubt. The entire built-up area of the town of Cassino and the Benedictine abbey on the heights above were destroyed by Allied bombing raids and artillery-fire prior to the attack by elements of the 4th Indian and 2nd New Zealand Infantry Divisions during the Second Battle for Cassino on 15–18 February 1944. The rubble hindered Allied armour supporting infantrymen and created optimal concealed Nazi defensive positions, such as the one above, to rain fire upon Freyberg's units. (USAMHI)

A US 34th Division military policeman directs traffic from a roadside dugout amid the rubble north of the town of Cassino in late January 1944. Elements of the 34th Division came within 1,000 yards of the Benedictine abbey. However, German counter-attacks compelled the exhausted Americans to retreat. (*USAMHI*)

A British soldier at Anzio digs a deep trench while his two mates sit upon the lip of the earthen field fortification. The trench's location was crucial as the beachhead's low water table led to endless flooding. (*Author's Collection*)

A hastily erected line of communication trenches and earthen pillboxes constructed by British troops at Anzio. The open areas between the beachhead and the Alban Hills offered little cover and such defences from Nazi artillery and air attacks had to be created. (*NARA*)

Two Royal Engineers of the 102nd Field Company clear a passageway beneath Nettuno's surface at Allied VI Corps headquarters' 'caves'. High calibre Nazi artillery shells were able to pierce through 30 feet of earth and stone. (*USAMHI*)

(**Opposite, above**) American soldiers finish a 0.30-inch calibre machine-gun outpost in the open plain beyond the Anzio–Nettuno beachhead. A slit trench was first dug then covered with corrugated steel and reinforced with earth. (*NARA*)

(**Opposite, below**) An American 40mm Bofors anti-aircraft gun and its crew in a sand-bagged enclosure at Anzio. The AA gun was deployed among other weapons such as barrage balloons and heavier ordnance to combat *Luftwaffe* attacks of the beachhead. (*NARA*)

(**Above**) After the Benedictine abbey's capture atop Monte Cassino in May 1944, a British soldier peers through a surviving window portal that served as a German observation post to direct artillery-fire onto Allied movements below. The thickness of the monastery's walls protected the Nazi defenders against Allied aerial and artillery bombardment from mid-February onwards. (*NARA*)

(**Opposite, above**) American combat engineers search for German landmines along a demolished roadway through the town of Cassino after the Nazis withdrew from the Gustav Line on 17 May 1944. After detection, land-mines were dug out by the engineers' careful bayonet probing and then defused. (*NARA*)

(**Opposite, below**) US Army engineers excavate stone buildings' outside walls in order to remove explosive booby traps placed by the departing Nazis in Anzio prior to Operations Shingle's D-Day on 22 January 1944. (*USAMHI*)

An American Combat Engineer examines a German *Tellermine* discovered with a metal detector upon a stone wall in the Cassino sector. The word *teller* in German meant dish, which described the shape of the 12-inch-wide by 3-inch-tall landmine. (*NARA*)

(**Opposite, above**) A US Army engineer attaches a length of wire to a German *Tellermine* after excavation. A simple pulley mechanism enabled lifting the landmine from a safe distance for defusing. The engineers contended with booby traps on the mines themselves, which would detonate the device during any attempted disarming by simply unscrewing the pressure plate or the screw cap. Over 3 million *Tellermines* of different types were produced from 1943–1944. (*NARA*)

(**Opposite, below**) British infantrymen with digging tools and censored insignia observe an M4 medium tank traverse a corridor cleared of mines over an otherwise innocuous small waterway, as indicated by the white tape markers. (*NARA*)

(**Above**) Near Castelforte, on the northern side of the Garigliano River, in May 1944, an American soldier examines the devastating effect of an exploded *Tellermine* to an Allied M4 medium tank's track and bogey wheels. Because of the mine's high operating pressure for detonation, only a heavy vehicle passing over it would set it off. (*USAMHI*)

(**Opposite, above**) A Polish Vickers machine-gun crew from the 3rd Carpathian Division atop some mountainous terrain on 27 March 1944 after the failed II New Zealand Corps attack at the Third Battle for Cassino. These infantrymen fighting in the Polish II Corps wore standard British battledress and used British Army equipment and weapons. Troops from this division were to partake in the attack along Snakeshead Ridge during the Fourth Battle for Cassino in mid-May. (*NARA*)

(**Opposite, below**) A Canadian infantryman examines a 2.75-pound shaped charge for his Projectile Infantry Anti-Tank (PIAT) weapon off to the right. The PIAT weighed 33 pounds and was touted as being able to penetrate 4 inches of armour with the force of a 75mm gun. A PIAT team usually comprised two soldiers and provided an Allied platoon with an effective, close-range anti-tank weapon that was also utilised against enemy fortified bunkers. (*NARA*)

(**Above**) A British Projectile Infantry Anti-Tank (PIAT) team (*right foreground*) fires their explosive charge at a target down a length of Italian road. The PIAT made its combat debut in Sicily during the summer of 1943 and gave small British infantry units the ability to combat armoured vehicles and fortified enemy positions. (*NARA*)

(**Opposite, above**) An 81mm mortar crew of the 3rd Battalion, 504th Parachute Infantry Regiment loads a round in their sandbag-lined weapon pit to fire on Nazi positions in the Cisterna area of the Anzio beachhead. The paratroopers manned the far right of the Allied perimeter at Anzio near the Mussolini Canal. (*NARA*)

(**Opposite, below**) A New Zealand 3-inch mortar crew amid the rubble of the town of Cassino created by Allied aerial and artillery bombardment. During the Second Battle for Cassino that occurred in mid-February 1944, the II New Zealand Corps' attacked with its 28th Maori Battalion, supported by the 2nd and 5th New Zealand Brigades, from the western bank of the Rapido towards the south-east of the town of Cassino toward the railway station. Elements of the 4th Indian Division's 7th Indian Brigade moved over the heights to the west of the town and Castle Hill and below the Benedictine abbey upon Monte Cassino. (*USAMHI*)

(**Opposite, above**) A British M2 4.2-inch mortar crew covers their ears as they fire on Cassino in the spring of 1944. The M2 was an improvement over the M1 Chemical Mortar and entered service in early 1943. Its 4-foot tube, weighing 105 pounds, was rifled and the weapon had a range of 560 to 4,400 yards. The M2 was suitable for the mountainous terrain of Italy as it delivered plunging fire rather than direct bombardment onto enemy positions often situated along reverse slopes. (*NARA*)

(**Opposite, below**) A British Ordnance QF (Quick-Firing) 6-pounder anti-tank gun crew from Eighth Army's 78th Division of XIII Corps, which had been transferred to the Cassino front, fires its weapons against Nazi enemy fortified strongpoints in Sant' Angelo south of Cassino and south-west of Monte Trocchio as part of Operation Diadem, to break through the Gustav Line in mid-May 1944. The term '6-pounder' referred to the weight of the gun's projectile. (*NARA*)

(**Above**) A British Ordnance QF (Quick-Firing) 17-pounder (76mm) anti-tank gun, towed by a truck being manually pushed out of deep mud during the winter of 1943–44. The 17-pounder had made its combat debut in Tunisia in 1943, in an attempt to have an effective AT gun against the German Panzer VI 'Tiger' tanks. (*NARA*)

(**Opposite, above**) A trio of British M3 75mm Gun Motor Carriage (GMC) self-propelled guns (SPG) fires from under camouflaged positions on the Cassino front near Sant' Angelo during the last week of February 1944. These SPGs initially saw combat during the Tunisian Campaign to replace the obsolete 37mm GMC. (*NARA*)

(**Above**) A British 'Bishop' self-propelled gun (SPG) is shown in profile with its armour-protected 25-pounder field gun mounted on a Valentine tank chassis to give its crew of four some shelter from high explosive (HE) enemy rounds. The Bishop first appeared in service in North Africa and continued to see action on Sicily and the Italian mainland. Its major deficiencies were its slow road speed as well as a limited gun elevation and traverse. However, it had a fording and vertical obstacle-clearing capability of about 3 feet. (*USAMHI*)

(**Opposite, below**) A Royal Artillery (RA) crew fires its Ordnance QF (Quick-Firing) 3.7-inch heavy anti-aircraft gun in an uncharacteristic field artillery or 'air burst' manner. Controversy existed over the under-utilisation of this weapon in counter-battery, counter-mortar or anti-tank roles akin to the German use of their dual-purpose 88mm FLAK. Nonetheless, the 3.7-inch guns were used effectively in a field artillery role in Italy. (*NARA*)

(**Opposite, above**) At the Nettuno beachhead, a US 90mm anti-aircraft gun crew from Battery C of the 68th Coast AA Artillery unit fires on German troop concentrations in early March 1944 when not staving off *Luftwaffe* aerial sorties. Both combatant sides frequently utilised AA artillery in a field artillery capacity. (*USAMHI*)

(**Opposite, below**) A smoke plume with a distinctive ring (*left*) from one of the guns of a British 4.5-inch medium artillery battery from the camouflaged weapon pits of E Troop of the 140th Medium Regiment, Royal Artillery, fires on the town of Cassino from the south on 8 March 1944, days prior to the start of the Third Battle for Cassino. Before the II New Zealand attacked the town of Cassino again, a massive Allied bombing raid, along with Allied artillery-fire, reduced the entire area to rubble. Unfortunately, this created excellent redoubts for the Nazi defenders and hampered the movement of supporting armour. (*USAMHI*)

(**Above**) A French–Lebanese colonial unit loads a shell into the breach of a US 155mm 'Long Tom' cannon during the last week of April 1944. The Long Tom was based on a First World War French cannon design. At this time, the French Expeditionary Corps (FEC) had been moved from the area north of Cassino to one stretching from Sant Ambrogio in the north to Castelforte in the south. For the mid-May 1944 Operation Diadem, the FEC's four divisions were to attack through the Aurunci Mountains and then sweep into the Liri Valley behind the Gustav Line. (*NARA*)

(**Above**) A 240mm Howitzer M1, also called the 'Black Dragon', of the US 97th Field Artillery Battalion in one of its combat debut fire missions at the end of January 1944 onto German positions from its camouflaged, sandbag-lined weapon pit in the Fifth Army sector near Mignano. This Howitzer was the most powerful weapon deployed by US field artillery units to penetrate heavily reinforced German targets with its 360-pound high-explosive shell ranging up to 25,000 yards. Prior to the Second Battle for Cassino, the 240mm Howitzer was used in the final destruction of the Benedictine abbey atop Monte Cassino after the massive aerial bombardment of the monastery on 15 February. (*USAMHI*)

(**Opposite, above**) A heavily camouflaged armoured column of M4 medium tanks of the I Canadian Corps in concentration for its role in Operation *Diadem* in May 1944 opposite Cassino once a breakthrough across the Gustav Line was achieved. This Canadian Corps comprised the 1st Infantry and 5th Armoured Divisions. (*NARA*)

(**Opposite, below**) An M10 3-inch Gun Motor Carriage Tank Destroyer completely dug-in as a static ordnance emplacement along the Cassino Front in early 1944. Mountainous terrain, narrow twisting roads and valleys all combined to compartmentalise the Italian battlefield, which often relegated Allied armour to a self-propelled artillery role. (*USAMHI*)

(**Above**) On the flat terrain within the Anzio–Nettuno beachhead, an American artillery-spotter uses a binocular periscope to observe approaching enemy while having some cover from German machine-gun or mortar fire. Quickly locating enemy armoured movements was essential to co-ordinate beachhead perimeter and offshore naval artillery gunfire. (*NARA*)

(**Opposite, above**) A team of US Army radar men are shown operating their Signal Corps Radio (SCR) 268 set to provide early warning to anti-aircraft defences in the Nettuno area. This was the US Army's first radar system, with an antennae cross-arm that was 40 feet wide and 10 feet high. The three operators sit on a pedestal atop a larger platform base. Both the antennae cross-arms and the pedestal had rotating capability to maximise ascertaining enemy aircraft distance and altitude. (*USAMHI*)

(**Opposite, below**) A *Luftwaffe* Heinkel (He)-111 twin-engined bomber on 25 January 1944 after it was shot down the night before during a raid on the Allied perimeter at Anzio. Updated models of the He-111 provided for an anti-shipping attack role. Field-Marshal Albert Kesselring placed confidence in his *Luftwaffe* to keep the Allied forces contained by bombing their transports with conventional bombers as well as with guided weapons that had proved to be very effective in their combat debut at Salerno. (*Author's Collection*)

(**Opposite, above**) A masonry Italian farmhouse is shown in the Anzio sector in April 1944. These stone structures had been modified into Nazi fortresses with machine-guns, light artillery pieces and mortars. Fortified buildings were also prized by the Allied troops to serve as observation posts, so competing infantry assaults to seize them were commonplace. This farmhouse, near Ceretto Alto, was stormed and captured by elements of the Canadian–American 1st Special Service Force, which had been transferred to the Anzio sector after their successful assaults against Nazi-defended mountain peaks, such as Monte la Difensa, in December 1943. (*USAMHI*)

(**Opposite, below**) In a village near the town of Cassino in February 1944, an American soldier removes an enemy machine-gun from a street-level house opening that served as a pillbox housed in an Italian stone structure. (*NARA*)

(**Above**) After the capture of Cisterna in May 1944 during the Anzio break-out, an American soldier carefully examines a Nazi trench for any lurking sniper or straggler. German equipment, ammunition boxes, stick grenades and an anti-tank magnetic explosive device are shown on the trench's surface. (*NARA*)

(**Opposite, above**) An Allied soldier inspects a shelled sunken Nazi tank turret, *Panzerturm*, which was incorporated into the more substantial Gustav and Hitler Lines, Most of the *Panzerturm* field fortifications were constructed with the turrets of disabled Panzer Mk V (Panther) tanks. (*NARA*)

(**Opposite, below**) A Nazi steel pillbox houses a machine-gun as an Allied soldier inspects it along the Gustav Line in the Cassino sector. (*NARA*)

(**Above**) At a roadside along the Cassino front, two American soldiers inspect portable metal pillboxes. These temporary structures were submerged into the terrain with German machine-gunners able to fire their weapons through the apertures at ground level. (*USAMHI*)

A captured German 20mm quadruple-barrelled *Flakvierling* 38 anti-aircraft gun being operated by a US 3rd Infantry Division soldier on the Anzio Front in 1944. This 20mm gun entered service in 1940 and proved to be one of the most effective German light AA weapons. A 37mm *Flakvierling* 43 entered service in 1944. (NARA)

An American soldier near Terracina in late May 1944 examines a German 88mm FLAK ordnance piece that was utilised in anti-tank, anti-aircraft and field artillery roles. This Nazi weapon earned the utmost respect among the Allies for its destructive capability. (*USAMHI*)

A *Püppchen* 88mm anti-tank rocket launcher is displayed after its capture in the Cisterna area in May 1944. It was the first of its kind captured by the Allies. One of the gun's projectiles stands in front of the wheel. (*USAMHI*)

(**Opposite, above**) A German coastal gun silenced by Fifth Army artillery in late May 1944 during Operation Diadem at Gaeta. Large calibre Nazi coastal ordnance, such as this weapon, led to the Allied naval planners' avoidance of an Italian mainland invasion in the Gulf of Gaeta in September 1943 and opting for less heavily defended beaches at Salerno. (*NARA*)

(**Opposite, below**) A disabled German Panzer VI 'Tiger' tank at Cisterna on 24 May 1944. This tank, first introduced during the Tunisian Campaign, had the extremely effective 88mm turret gun. To deal with its tank-destroying capability, the British developed the 17-pounder anti-tank gun. (*USAMHI*)

(**Above**) A disabled 70-ton German 88mm self-propelled gun (SPG) or tank destroyer, called Ferdinand after its designer Ferdinand Porsche, is shown after capture by the Allies in the Cisterna area. Less than 100 of these armoured vehicles were built in 1942–43, after a hurried development for deployment at the Battle of Kursk in July 1943. There, it had a high killing ratio of roughly 10:1 due to the range of its 88mm gun. However, lack of a defensive machine-gun and poor turret visibility made it vulnerable to Soviet infantry placing explosive charges. In addition to mechanical failure, slow speed and large size made them easy targets for Russian gunners. In September 1943, all Kursk battlefield-surviving Ferdinands were withdrawn to Italy. Fitted with a machine-gun in the hull to combat infantry as well as commander's cupola for improved vision. This modification was renamed the *Elefant*. In Italy, persistent mechanical failure and massive weight, which limited them from most local roads and bridges, were major operational detriments. (*USAMHI*)

(**Opposite, above**) Two Moroccan soldiers of the French Expeditionary Corps view a German small calibre self-propelled gun (SPG) buried under the rubble of Castelforte on 13 May 1944. All along the Gustav Line, German SPGs were used in a static artillery role due to terrain limitations. (*NARA*)

(**Above**) An American soldier sits upon a captured Nazi self-propelled gun, the *Marder* ('Marten') III tank destroyer, near Castellonorato in mid-May 1944. The *Marder* III's main armament was the Soviet 76.2mm 1936 divisional field gun that was mounted in an open-topped turret on the chassis of the Czechoslovak LT-38 tank. The *Marder* III offered limited crew protection from enemy artillery-fire, but provided significant firepower. (*USAMHI*)

(**Opposite, below**) A German self-propelled gun (SPG) with a 150mm Howitzer, called the *Hummel* ('Bumble Bee'), is shown after its capture outside Cisterna on 24 May 1944. The open-turreted gun was situated atop a Panzer IV tank chassis and was a major component of the heavy artillery of Panzer and *panzergrenadier* divisions. Alternatively, an 88mm anti-tank gun was also deployed with this SPG design. (*USAMHI*)

(**Opposite, above**) American infantrymen at the Anzio beachhead examine a *Neger* one-man torpedo that was utilised against Allied offshore shipping. These anti-shipping weapons were operated *en masse* by K-Flotilla 175 *Neger* submarines during the third week of April 1944. (*NARA*)

(**Above**) Four New Zealanders fire a captured German 75mm *Panzerabwehrkanone* (PaK) 40 against Nazi machine-gun positions on the heights of Monte Cassino above them during the Second Battle for Cassino in mid-February 1944. The PaK 40 was introduced into German service in February 1942. Although very effective, its excessive weight necessitated towing and hastened the development of self-propelled guns, such as the *Marder*, within *Wehrmacht* formations. (*NARA*)

(**Opposite, below**) Canadian troops inspect two five-barrelled German *Nebelwerfers* or rocket launchers. These weapons were used with devastating effect against attacking troops of the II New Zealand Corps as they advanced through the gullies and hillsides during their approach to Monastery Hill at the Third Battle for Cassino. (*NARA*)

Chapter Three

Commanders and Combatants

As mid-February 1944 approached, the First Battle for Cassino ended with General Clark's Fifth Army contained by the German Tenth Army, under General Heinrich von Vietinghoff, along a 25-mile sector running from Monte Cassino to the Tyrrhenian Sea. After an unopposed landing of US VI Corps, under Major-General John Lucas, at Anzio, 30 miles south of Rome on 22 January, a rapidly deployed German Fourteenth Army, under General Eberhard von Mackensen, prevented an Allied offensive from its perimeter on 30 January. In addition, Mackensen launched violent counter-attacks during the first three weeks of February against the Allied positions at Anzio subjecting them to a siege.

In the central and southern sectors of the Gustav Line, the German Tenth Army fielded the equivalent of nine divisions that were divided into two regular and one provisional corps. The XIV Panzer Corps was under General Fridolin von Senger und Etterlin and held the area from the Tyrrhenian Sea across the Aurunci Mountains to the Liri Valley. The German 94th Infantry Division was along the coast while the 71st Infantry Division was inland at the Montes Maio–Faito massif. Between the 71st Infantry Division and the Liri River were detachments from the 15th and 29th Panzer Grenadier Divisions, among other units.

The *Wehrmacht's* LI Mountain Corps, commanded by General Valentin Feuerstein, was stationed further inland and comprised the 44th Infantry Division in the Liri Valley, and the 1st Parachute Division continued to hold the Monte Cassino sector. To the north of the Monte Cairo massif, the German 5th Mountain and the 144th Jäger Division, comprising the LI Mountain Corps' left wing, joined with a provisional corps, *Gruppe Hauck*, commanded by General Friedrich Hauck, which was situated in a relatively inactive sector between the Pescara River and the Adriatic Sea. It comprised the 305th and 334th Infantry Divisions.

At Anzio, Mackensen's Fourteenth Army initially comprised the I Parachute Corps, under General Alfred Schlemm, and then the LXXVI Panzer Corps, under General Traugott Herr. On the morning of the Allied landings at Anzio, Kesselring ordered the 4th Parachute Division, which was just activated to the north of Rome, to now get situated on the Tyrrhenian coast, along with some replacement units of the Hermann Göring Division, to control the roads from the beachhead to the Alban Hills and to

Rome. Nazi headquarters in Berlin also directed the 715th Infantry Division from Avignon in the South of France to Italy, along with other garrison units from the Balkans. A new division, the 92nd Infantry, was to be raised from replacement units in northern Italy and directed to Anzio. Additionally, major elements of the 65th Infantry Division (stationed at Genoa) and the 362nd Infantry Division (garrisoned at Rimini) were to move to the new Allied beachhead immediately. From the Cassino Front, General Vietinghoff complied with Kesselring's urgent appeal for troops and sent elements from some of his divisions, notably the 71st Infantry and 29th Panzer Grenadier formations. Kesselring was masterful at moving other German units into the Anzio cauldron from quieter zones along the Gustav Line and from the south of Rome.

Lucas, the US VI Corps commander for the Anzio landings, led a variety of American and British formations on 22 January 1944. These included: the British 1st Division, accompanied by the 2nd Special Service Brigade (SSB) of the Nos. 9 and 43 Royal Marine (RM) Commandos, on the left flank of the beachhead south of the Moletta River, the US 3rd Infantry Division, plus the 1st, 3rd and 4th Ranger Battalions, the 504th Parachute Infantry Regiment and the 509th Parachute Infantry Battalion of the US 82nd Airborne Division securing Anzio, Nettuno and bridges along the western branch of the Mussolini Canal to secure the beachhead's right flank. The Allied perimeter was 7 miles deep and 16 miles long.

As the siege of the Anzio perimeter continued, Major-General Lucian Truscott took over command of the US VI Corps on 22 February 1944. He received additional reinforcements, including the British 5th Division, the US 34th and 45th Infantry Divisions, and Combat Command A (CCA) of the US 1st Armoured Division. Also, the Allied beachhead received the US 36th Combat Engineer Regiment and Brigadier Robert Frederick's Canadian–American 1st Special Service Force (SSF), a regiment-sized elite mountain-experienced unit. General Clark held the veteran but bloodied US 36th Infantry Division in Fifth Army reserve, but it too was to be sent to Anzio.

For the Second and Third Battles for Cassino, in mid-February and mid-March respectively, the *ad hoc* II New Zealand Corps, under General Bernard Freyberg, comprised the 2nd New Zealand, the 4th Indian, and the 78th British Infantry Divisions as well a combat group of the US 1st Armoured Division. These Eighth Army formations were moved from the quiet Adriatic Front across the Apennines to Cassino in late January to early February 1944 to reinforce the exhausted US 34th and 36th Divisions' regiments of II Corps that had gained a foothold across the Rapido River north and west of the town during the First Battle for Cassino.

For action, before and during the Fourth and final Battle for Cassino, as part of Operation Diadem in mid-May 1944, the Polish II Corps, under Lieutenant-General Wladyslaw Anders, fielded the 3rd Carpathian Rifles and 5th Kresowa Infantry Divisions and the 2nd Armoured Brigade.

Beginning in March 1944, General Alexander's staff concluded that the Liri Valley, situated between the western slopes of the Central Apennines and the Anzio beachhead, was the only suitable terrain for a mid-May offensive, Operation Diadem. Here, Allied armour and air assets could be utilised to their utmost capabilities. For this attack to break through the Gustav Line and beyond, Clark's Fifth Army, now comprising two US II Corps divisions, under Major-General Geoffrey Keyes, and four FEC divisions, under General Alphonse Juin, was to be shifted to the narrower corridor between the Liri Valley and the Tyrrhenian Sea. Their attack was to move along the coast and through the Aurunci Mountains.

US II Corps fielded two newly arrived infantry divisions, the 85th and 88th, commanded by Major-Generals John Coulter and John Sloan respectively. These two divisions were the first American infantry divisions, comprised mostly of draftees to enter combat. Beginning in early April, the 85th Division took over the Minturno bridgehead, while the 88th Division was inland and became the left flank of the FEC. Both of the American divisions took over the sector previously occupied by the combat-depleted British X Corps under General Richard McCreery, which was transferred to a less active front across the Central Apennines' desolate wilderness to become the re-located Eighth Army's right wing.

The FEC, armed and equipped by the US Army, became the right flank of US II Corps, after incurring almost 8,000 casualties in an attempt to envelop Monte Cassino from the north with the US 34th Infantry Division in late January to early February 1944. French mountain troops from this corps showed their combat ability by seizing Montes Belvedere and Abate during this offensive. During early April, the FEC comprised the 4th Moroccan Mountain, the 2nd Moroccan and 3rd Algerian Infantry, and the French 1st Motorised Infantry Divisions, the latter including many Free French recruits.

The central sector of the Gustav Line was assigned to General Oliver Leese's Eighth Army divisions, which had moved across the Central Apennines to forward positions opposite Cassino. British V Corps, under General Charles Allfrey, maintained responsibility for containing the Germans along the entire less-active Adriatic Sea sector and was available to pursue any enemy withdrawal from this area. The Eighth Army's striking force for Operation Diadem comprised British XIII Corps, under Lieutenant-General Sidney Kirkman, which fielded four infantry divisions: the British 4th, 78th and Indian 8th formations as well as the British 6th Armoured Division, situated across the Rapido River opposite the entrance to the Liri Valley. The I Canadian Corps, under Major-General E.L.M. Burns, comprised the Canadian 1st Infantry and 5th Armoured Divisions. This corps was held in reserve for the breakthrough into the Liri Valley. The South African 6th Armoured Division was also a reserve formation.

Both Allied Fifth and Eighth Armies were multinational formations. The US Fifth Army reflected the coalitions of America, Britain and France. The British Eighth Army was even more polyglot with expatriate soldiers from Poland, Belgium, Greece and Yugoslavia. The core formations from the United Kingdom and the British Commonwealth included Canadians, New Zealanders, South Africans, Indians and Nepalese. Italy, as a recent ally after the September capitulation, provided a motorised group and some artillery units.

The troop dispositions above had been arrayed for two separate battles: along the length of the Gustav Line and within the congested Allied beachhead at Anzio. Manpower issues were important for both combatants. The Allies siphoned off men, supplies and shipping for the upcoming Normandy invasion on 6 June 1944, relegating the MTO to a backwater in the minds of some Allied commanders. For Germany, soon to be fighting on three fronts, attrition and a lack of replacements plagued Kesselring, especially after the failed Fourteenth Army counter-offensive at Anzio by the third week of February 1944.

General Dwight D. Eisenhower (*left*), Supreme Allied Commander, MTO, talks with British prime minister Winston Churchill, with General Harold Alexander, commanding general of the Allied 15th Army Group, behind them, in Marrakech on Christmas Day 1943. Churchill, an advocate for the upcoming Anzio assault, was recovering from pneumonia; hence the dragon-covered robe over his siren suit. Eisenhower was soon to become the commander of the Supreme Headquarters Allied Expeditionary Force (SHAEF) based in London, with British General Henry Maitland Wilson succeeding him at the helm of the MTO. (*Author's Collection*)

General Harold Alexander (*right*), then commander-in-chief, Middle East, with Major-General A. John Harding (*left*), commanding general of the British 7th Armoured Division, seen standing in the rear of a staff car in the North African desert in 1942. Alexander was a highly decorated and wounded First World War veteran, who witnessed the final phase of the Dunkirk evacuation as British I Corps commander. Then he oversaw the ignoble retreat across Burma to India in the spring of 1942 in the face of the Japanese juggernaut across Asia. In August 1942, he succeeded Auchinleck as commander-in-chief, Middle East, and provided strategic oversight for Montgomery's re-vitalised Eighth Army for the victory at El Alamein in November 1942 and the movement across North Africa into south-eastern Tunisia. Like Eisenhower, Alexander was not renowned for any grand strategic ability. However, he was capable of uniting fractious Allied generals into a common purpose of defeating the Nazis in Italy. Harding was wounded in North Africa and, upon recovery, became Alexander's chief of staff in January 1944. Harding was instrumental in the planning and execution of Operation Diadem, which cracked the Nazi Gustav Line in mid-May 1944. (*Author's Collection*)

Lieutenant-General Mark W. Clark (*right*), commanding general of US Fifth Army, and his G-3, Brigadier-General Donald Brann (*left*), in transit aboard a US Navy Patrol Torpedo (PT) boat from their rear echelon headquarters to the Anzio front in early February 1944. Clark was a West Point graduate and a wounded combat veteran of the First World War. Like his close friend Eisenhower, Clark too had a meteoric rise in military rank, becoming the youngest lieutenant-general in the US Army at the age of 46 during Operation Torch in November 1942, where he liaised with Vichy French leaders, such as Admiral Darlan, to broker an armistice in north-west Africa. In December 1942, he assumed command of the headquarters of the US Fifth Army and led its American and British formations into combat during the near-disastrous invasion of the Italian mainland at Salerno in September 1943. Clark exuded valour and was no stranger to the Allied battlefields. In December 1944, he succeeded Alexander as commander of the Allied 15th Army Group, when the latter was promoted to supreme commander of the Armed Forces Headquarters in the Mediterranean, replacing Field-Marshal Henry Maitland Wilson. (*NARA*)

The principal Allied military leaders at Anzio in early 1944. From left-to-right they include: Major-General Lucian Truscott, commanding general of the US 3rd Infantry Division; General Harold Alexander, commander Allied 15th Army Group; Lieutenant-General Mark W. Clark, commanding general US Fifth Army; an unidentified staff officer; and Major-General John P. Lucas, commanding general of US VI Corps. Lucas graduated from West Point in 1911 and was severely wounded in France in 1918. He commanded the US 3rd Infantry Division during the initial entry of the Americans into the Second World War and, in 1942–43, was promoted to command the US III Corps. During the Sicily invasion, Lucas served as Eisenhower's liaison officer to Lieutenant-General Patton's Seventh Army. Following the abrupt relief of Major-General Ernest Dawley after the Salerno battles ended, Lucas took over the blooded US VI Corps that had comprised the 36th and 45th Infantry Divisions. Throughout the terrible weather during autumn of 1943, a soon-to-be exhausted Lucas led VI Corps through the horrific Italian mountainous terrain to gain access to the Rapido River along the Nazi Gustav Line. Lucas had voiced extreme scepticism of the Anzio amphibious assault and penned privately in his diary that Churchill's meddling might reproduce the 'strong odour of Gallipoli', referring to the failed Allied Dardanelles assault on the Turkish coast in 1915. (USAMHI)

General Henry Maitland Wilson (*centre*) with Major-General Geoffrey Keyes (*right*), commanding general of US II Corps, in Italy in May 1944. Wilson had the longest experience in the MTO, having arrived in Egypt in 1939 to serve as general officer commanding (GOC), Egypt under General Archibald Wavell, commander-in-chief (CIC), Middle East. He played successful roles in both Operation Compass in 1940–41 and in Syria. However, he was also involved in the debacle in Greece and then Crete. Nonetheless, he enjoyed the confidence of Churchill. Wilson became the supreme commander MTO and was supportive of Operation Shingle, the amphibious assault at Anzio on 22 January 1944. In December 1944, Churchill promoted Wilson as head of the British Military Mission in Washington and awarded him a field-marshal's baton. Geoffrey Keyes was a West Point graduate, a veteran cavalryman, and regarded as an 'intellectual soldier'. Prior to being the deputy commander of US Seventh Army, under Patton, during the invasion of Sicily, Keyes was his mentor's deputy in I Armoured Corps in north-west Africa after Bradley assumed command of US II Corps in Tunisia. After the 3rd Infantry Division captured Agrigento with Patton's famous 'reconnaissance in force', Keyes commanded a provisional corps in Sicily, which captured Palermo on 22 July 1943 after moving on this objective only a few days previously. In January 1944, Keyes led II Corps' 34th and 36th Infantry Divisions, the former crossing the Rapido River north of Cassino and almost succeeding in capturing the monastery in early February, while the latter had two of its regiments decimated during its Rapido assault south of the town on 20–22 January 1944. For Operation Diadem in May 1944, Keyes commanded the newly arrived US 85th and 88th Infantry Divisions. (*NARA*)

(**Left**) Lieutenant-General Jacob L. Devers, Deputy Supreme Commander MTO, decorates Lieutenant-General Ladislaw (Wladyslaw) Anders in August 1944 for his gallant leadership and fighting *élan* of the Polish II Corps. Within weeks, Devers led the Allied 6th Army Group, US Seventh and 1st French Armies in the invasion of southern France. In 1939, Anders was a Polish brigade commander and was captured by the Soviets. After being imprisoned for a year, he was released to form a unit comprising Polish prisoners-of-war in the Soviet Union that their captors did not want to arm. After a lengthy odyssey from Russia to the Middle East, the Polish II Corps was armed and trained by the British. In early 1944, the Polish II Corps was sent to Italy. (*NARA*)

(**Right**) French Expeditionary Corps (FEC) commanding general Alphonse Juin in 1944. Juin was captured by the Nazis in May 1940. The Vichy French regime installed him as commander-in-chief of the French North African Army. However, he quickly joined the Allies soon after the Operation Torch landings in November 1942. Juin led his FEC mountain warriors from the Maghreb with great military tactical skill and *élan* during the First Battle for Cassino in late January–early February 1944, and successfully crossed the Rapido River north of the town and monastery. He criticised Fifth Army commanders for not committing II New Zealand Corps to the assault, which might have enabled the FEC and the US 34th Division to swing south behind the German positions and into the Liri Valley, thereby outflanking the Gustav Line during the First Battle for Cassino. Later under his command, the four FEC divisions adroitly moved through the Montes Maio–Faito massif during Operation Diadem, contributing greatly to the breakthrough of the Gustav Line in mid-May 1944. (*NARA*)

General Oliver Leese, commanding general British Eighth Army, shakes hands with Lieutenant-General Bernard Freyberg, commander II New Zealand Corps near Cassino. Leese led British XXX Corps from El Alamein in August 1942 throughout the Sicilian campaign. Leese took over Eighth Army in late December 1943 when his mentor, Montgomery, departed for England to plan the Normandy land campaign. Freyberg was a Victoria Cross-decorated veteran of the First World War. After his defeat on Crete in 1941, Freyberg led the 2nd New Zealand Division as part of Eighth Army throughout North Africa. For the Second Battle for Cassino, under Clark's Fifth Army, Freyberg commanded the II New Zealand Corps, comprising his 2nd New Zealand and 4th Indian Infantry Divisions. (NARA)

(**Above**) Lieutenant-General Henry D.G. Crerar, commanding general I Canadian Corps, congratulates junior officers from a regiment of the 1st Canadian Tank Brigade. Crerar led the I Canadian Corps from August 1942 to March 1944. The I Canadian Corps comprised the 1st Canadian Infantry and the 5th Canadian Armoured Divisions along with the 1st Canadian Tank Brigade. The Canadians were to be a major attacking force up the Liri Valley at the end of May 1944 after the breakthrough of the Gustav Line. (*NARA*)

(**Opposite, above**) I Canadian Corps commanding general Lieutenant-General Eedson L. Burns talks with Major-General Chris Vokes, commanding general 1st Canadian Infantry Division. Burns, an intellectual officer, led the Canadians during the Liri Valley campaign against the Hitler Line following the collapse of the Gustav Line in mid-May 1944. However, he had difficulties interacting with both his British commanders and subordinate Canadian divisional leaders. (*NARA*)

(**Opposite, below**) The US VI Corps commanding general for the Anzio invasion, Major John P. Lucas (*centre*) with Rear-Admiral T. Troutbridge, RN, and Major-General William R.C. Penney, commanding general British 1st Infantry Division, aboard HMS *Bulolo* prior to the landings of 22 January 1944. On 10 February, after the Nazi counter-attacks commenced on the Allies, Penney became incensed over Lucas's ambivalence about his division's infantry casualties around the tenuous Carroceto salient. (*Author's Collection*)

Major-General Francis Tuker, commander II New Zealand Corps' 4th Indian Infantry Division. He was adept at mountain warfare having led Gurkhas during the First World War, along the interwar Indian Frontier, and in Ethiopia. Commanding this division since 1941, he argued with his corps and senior Allied commanders to bomb the Benedictine abbey upon Monte Cassino on 15 February 1944 to protect his troops as he feared the Nazis were using the monastery as an observation post. Tuker became ill just before this Second Battle for Cassino and was evacuated. (*Author's Collection*)

Major-General Charles Ryder, commanding general US 34th Infantry Division. Ryder led this division, a National Guard unit comprising Mid-westerners from North and South Dakota, Iowa and Minnesota, ashore during Operation Torch in November 1942. Although elements of Ryder's 34th Division, as part of Keyes' US II Corps, had crossed the Rapido River north of the town of Cassino in late January to early February 1944 and were poised to capture the Benedictine monastery on the heights above, a failure to reinforce the division's exhausted regiments with elements of the II New Zealand Corps ended the First Battle for Cassino. However, the feat of arms by the battle-tested 34th Division was acclaimed. After re-fitting, the 34th Division subsequently re-deployed to Anzio in early March. (*NARA*)

The US 36th 'Texas' Infantry Division's commanding general Major-General Fred L. Walker. He was regarded as a highly competent regular army officer and led his division during the Salerno landings on 9 September 1943. Walker did not greatly admire his superior, Clark, especially after the tentative plan to evacuate the VI Corps beachhead during the Nazi counter-attack of 13 September 1943 and the failed Rapido River crossing by two of his division's regiments, as part of Keyes' US II Corps, on 20–22 January 1944. (*NARA*)

(**Left**) Colonel William O. Darby, then commanding officer US 157th Infantry Regiment of the 45th Division, being awarded a Distinguished Service Order by the British Eighth Army commander General Leese in April 1944. Darby was a West Point graduate who initially started soldiering as an officer in the army's last horse artillery unit. Darby commanded the ranger battalions that he formed in the United Kingdom in 1942, along with the training *élan* of the British Commandos. On 22 January 1944, at Anzio, Darby led ashore the US 6615th Ranger Group (Provisional) that comprised the 1st, 3rd and 4th Ranger Battalions, the 504th Parachute Infantry Regiment and the US 509th Parachute Infantry Battalion. General Truscott said of Darby: 'Never in this war have I known a more gallant, heroic officer'. (*USAMHI*)

(**Right**) General Harold Alexander, Allied 15th Army Group commander, talks informally with a group of Darby's US Rangers of the 6615th Ranger Force (Provisional) at Anzio shortly after the landings in late January 1944. In 1942, while undergoing rigorous training by British Commando officers in the United Kingdom, Truscott gave the initial group of this elite formation its moniker from Rogers Rangers, which had fought under the Crown as light infantry in the pre-Revolutionary American colonial battles against the French and their Indian tribe allies. Under Darby's leadership, ranger battalions fought in North Africa and on Sicily. At Salerno in early September 1943, Darby's Rangers were utilised in an elite capacity to seize and hold the important heights at the Chiunzi Pass, after landing at Maiori to the west of Salerno along the northern coast of the Gulf of Salerno in the British X Corps sector. However, at Anzio, of the 767 Rangers of the 1st and 3rd Battalions who spearheaded the US 3rd Division's assault on Cisterna on 30 January 1944, only six made it back to Allied lines with 450 captured and the rest killed by armoured elements of the Hermann Göring Division. (*NARA*)

Brigadier-General Robert T. Frederick, commanding officer Canadian–American 1st Special Service Force (SSF), shakes hands with US VI Corps commander, Major-General Lucas, at Nettuno in early 1944. As a colonel, Frederick led his 1st SSF in reconnaissance and raiding operations in Italy's mountainous terrain attached to Keyes' II Corps, notably at Monte la Difensa on 2 December 1943, during which the elite infantry unit incurred over 500 casualties including seventy-three killed in action while capturing that part of the massif. After participating in further mountain combat, Frederick's 1st SSF embarked for Anzio in February and amalgamated the surviving US 4th Ranger Battalion into his unit. For the break-out from the Anzio perimeter in late May 1944, the 1st SSF was to be the US 3rd Division's right flank. (*USAMHI*)

(**Opposite, above**) A heavily armed detachment of Brigadier-General Frederick's Canadian–American 1st Special Service Force on a 2 June 1944 patrol pursuing the retreating Germans after the Anzio break-out.. The patrol leader cradles a 0.45-inch calibre Thompson submachine-gun, while the second soldier carried a Johnson M1941 Light Machine-Gun (LMG). This weapon, also called a 'Johnny gun', was designed by Melvin Johnson Jr, a Boston-based lawyer and captain in the Marine Corps Reserve. The LMG was fed from a curved, single-column 25-round magazine attached to the left side of the receiver, which made it awkward to carry on patrol when loaded. This M1941 version had a wooden stock and a metal bipod and was able to fire at a rate of 200 to 600 rounds per minute. The third soldier in line shouldered an M9 Bazooka that fired a shaped charge warhead at short range against enemy armoured vehicles or pillboxes. Finally, the fourth infantryman holds a 'walkie-talkie', which was also named Set, Complete Radio or Signal Corps Radio (SCR)-536. This device was introduced for use by platoon and company communication, and under good conditions had a range of about a mile. With its fifty channels, the SCR-536 was the first hand-held portable radio system. (*NARA*)

(**Opposite, below**) American and British infantry in their respective landing craft move into Anzio Harbour during Operation Shingle on 22 January 1944. As the gradient of some of the Peter sector beaches in the British landing zone were too shallow for efficient unloading of troops and supplies, Lucas moved elements of British 1st Division's amphibious assault troops to Anzio Harbour. (*USAMHI*)

(**Above**) Private Victor Russo from the Headquarters Company, 171st Field Artillery (FA) Battalion, repairs a telephone line that was disrupted during a snowstorm in the Fifth Army's Cassino sector in early January 1944. The 171st FA Battalion was part of the US 45th Infantry Division and utilised truck-towed M2 A1 105mm Howitzers, the army's standard divisional artillery, and saw action in North Africa, Sicily, and Salerno. (*USAMHI*)

(**Opposite**) An American corporal from C Battery of the 697th Field Artillery (FA) Battalion wipes off shells at his camouflaged, sand-bagged weapon-pit before a fire mission in May 1944. This unit employed truck-towed 240mm M1 'Black Dragon' Howitzers and was deployed to Italy in January 1944 under US II Corps. The M1 Black Dragon was the most powerful weapon used and targeted Nazi heavy concrete fortifications. (*NARA*)

(**Opposite, above**) An American private within the Anzio perimeter sits atop his armoured vehicle near a 0.50-inch calibre machine-gun, receiving instructions from his battery headquarters commander. His communications device was a Set, Complete Radio (also called Signal Corps Radio) (SCR)-300 backpack radio with a telephone handset, which had a maximal range of 5 miles and was utilised at the battalion and company level, although most tanks and command Jeeps had radios built into them. (*USAMHI*)

(**Opposite, below**) At Monte Lungo, just to the south-east of the town of Cassino, near Highway 6, an American self-propelled anti-aircraft gun crew in the Allied Fifth Army is on alert for *Luftwaffe* air attacks. Situated at the rear of the tracked vehicle is a 37mm AA gun with twin 0.50-inch calibre machine-guns. (*NARA*)

(**Above**) During the harsh winter of 1944, the wet, cold climate took its toll on the feet of Allied infantrymen. Trench Foot was capable of crippling a soldier, due to infrequent sock-changing during static warfare in water-filled trenches. Here, newly arrived infantrymen from the US 337th Regiment, 85th Division, undergo bi-weekly foot inspection by medical orderlies for early detection to prevent casualties. (*USAMHI*)

(**Above**) At the Cassino sector of the Nazi Gustav Line along the Rapido River, signallers at a US 143rd Infantry Regiment message centre of the 36th Division try to stay warm and dry in a thick-walled converted pig-sty. (*USAMHI*)

(**Opposite, above**) Lieutenant-General Lucian Truscott inspects troops of the African–American 92nd 'Buffalo' Division, as indicated by their left shoulder patch insignia. This unit received numerous decorations and citations for combat gallantry in Italy. (*NARA*)

(**Opposite, below**) British Eighth Army infantrymen going 'over the top' of their trench against Nazi positions in the Cassino sector in May 1944. Both the British 4th and 78th Infantry Divisions of Lieutenant-General Sidney Kirkman's XIII Corps continued their pressure on the enemy south of the town of Cassino. On 15 May, elements of the 78th Division had cut the Cassino–Pignataro, which isolated Cassino from the Liri Valley. (*NARA*)

(**Above**) An Eighth Army Signals section takes cover within the ruins of the town in mid-March 1944 during the Third Battle for Cassino. Following another massive Allied aerial and artillery bombardment of Cassino on 15 March, Indian and New Zealand infantry battalions from Freyberg's II New Zealand Corps, accompanied by some armour, attacked both the town and Hill 193, Castle Hill. However, the remnants of the German 1st Parachute Division, under Major-General Richard Heidrich, were not dislodged from the ruins. The railway station and an area of hillocks just to the east of the Gari River and south of the town of Cassino were captured and held by the New Zealanders, despite Nazi counter-attacks. (*NARA*)

(**Opposite, above**) Unfavourable hydrographic gradients complicated the unloading of British transports at Task Force Peter's beaches at the start of the Anzio landings, while fierce weather erupted a few days later. Here, Royal Navy ratings and British Army sappers secure a portion of a pontoon bridge during rough seas and high surf amid gale-force winds on 24 January 1944. (*NARA*)

(**Opposite, below**) A British mortar crew fires an American 81mm mortar at night at enemy positions in the Anzio sector on 8 May 1944. Depending on the type of round fired, this infantry weapon, comprising a simple tube, bipod, baseplate and aiming sight, had a maximum range of 1,300 to 3,300 yards. (*USAMHI*)

312829

(**Above**) A British X Corps sapper, who was wounded in the face when an enemy mine exploded, is led to a rear area dressing station by stretcher-bearers (SBs) on the Garigliano River Front in early February 1944. The SBs wore armbands on their left arm below their leather jerkins to denote their status. (*NARA*)

An infantry section from the British X Corps passes the corpses of dead German troops on the Garigliano River Front in late January 1944. Lieutenant-General Richard McCreery's divisions, which sustained large infantry losses with the battles at Salerno, the movement north from Naples and across the Volturno River, the attacks on the Montes Camino–la Difensa massif, and the assault across the Garigliano River, were to be shifted east across the Apennine Mountains to a less active front as British Eighth Army divisions were to bolster Clark's Fifth Army on the Gustav Line. (NARA)

An Eighth Army infantry section moves through the town of Cassino in the vicinity of the Hotel de Roses in May 1944. This iconic photograph demonstrated the ruinous nature of the Allied aerial and artillery bombardment with a similarly devastated Castle Hill (background). (NARA)

(**Opposite, above**) British No. 9 Commandos sit in a Jeep with some of their German prisoners after a raid behind enemy lines in late December 1943, Operation Partridge. Their mission was to divert attention away from British X Corps movements for the upcoming crossing of the Garigliano River. Although there were some mishaps in the Commandos' landings along the northern shore of the Garigliano River estuary, approximately thirty Nazi prisoners were taken. (*NARA*)

(**Above**) Two Indian Army soldiers, a Sikh (*left*) and a Pathan (*right*), of British XIII Corps' 8th Indian Infantry Division, side-by-side manhandling a 6-pounder anti-tank gun prior to their Rapido River assault during Operation Diadem in mid-May 1944. An Indian division was two-thirds Indian and one-third British. Each division had three brigades consisting of one British and two Indian battalions. The term Pathan referred to the Pashtun-speaking people inhabiting northern India, principally from Kashmir, Bihar and the Punjab regions. The Sikh religion also originated in the Punjab region during the fifteenth century. The 8th Indian Division also comprised Gurkhas and British formations. (*NARA*)

(**Opposite, below**) A Universal Carrier with Indian reconnaissance troops from the 8th Indian Division advances as part of the British XIII Corps' breakthrough at the Gustav Line on 18 May 1944, one day after the Nazis withdrew from their Cassino entrenchments to avoid encirclement. During the early spring of 1944, the 8th Indian Division was re-deployed from the less active Adriatic coast sector west across the Apennine Mountains as part of Kirkman's XIII Corps south of the town of Cassino. (*NARA*)

(**Opposite, above**) At the Cassino Front, a Sikh soldier from one of the Punjab regiments of the Tuker's 4th Indian Infantry Division adjusts his turban in February 1944. Elements from this division were to fight in the Second and Third Battles for Cassino, attacking the various heights above the town leading to the Benedictine abbey. (*USAMHI*)

(**Above**) Gurkha infantrymen walk past a motorised column in single-file after crossing a river on their way to reach the front. These fierce Nepalese warriors, known for their mountain fighting ability, had fought in the Second, Third and Fourth Battles for Cassino as part of the 4th and 8th Indian Infantry Divisions of Eighth Army. On 18 February 1944, during the Second Battle for Cassino, some Gurkha companies from the 4th Indian Division advanced down the ravine below Monastery Hill from the north. However, when these troops tried to climb up to the Benedictine abbey upon Monte Cassino, they were repulsed by the Nazi defenders and incurred numerous casualties. (*NARA*)

(**Opposite, below**) Two Gurkha infantrymen in late March 1944 after the failed Third Battle for Cassino. Early on 16 March, companies from the 1/9th Gurkha Rifles of the 5th Indian Brigade established themselves on Hangman's Hill (Point 435) below the monastery. There they remained isolated for over a week under Nazi 1st Parachutist Battalion's machine-gunfire and mortar shelling. However, they were unable to reach the Benedictine abbey. (*NARA*)

(**Opposite, above**) Canadian reinforcements arrive in Italy in late January 1944. The 1st Canadian Infantry Division had been extensively bloodied in the Eighth Army's mountainous sector in the fall of 1943 and along the Adriatic Sea at the hellacious Battle of Ortona in late December. These reinforcements became part of I Canadian Corps, comprising the 1st Canadian Infantry and the 5th Canadian Armoured Divisions, along with the 1st Canadian Tank Brigade. (*NARA*)

(**Opposite, below**) Two Canadian soldiers from a signals unit hang a sign: Dust Draws Morter Fire Go Slow. With the Germans possessing the heights along the Cassino sector, road dust invited enemy shelling as it suggested large Allied motorised columns. (*NARA*)

(**Above**) A Canadian infantryman carrying extra Projector Infantry anti-tank rounds from the Cape Breton Highlanders trudges past a dead German on 26 May 1944. After the breakthrough at the Gustav Line, the I Canadian Corps was unleashed alongside British XIII Corps in the Liri Valley and pierced the Hitler Line at Pontecorvo on 23 May. Days later, they had to cross the Melfa River, which ran perpendicular to the Liri River north of the Hitler Line, against incomplete Nazi fortifications. (*NARA*)

Three New Zealand infantrymen from their 6th Infantry Brigade use the side of a ruined building as cover as they manoeuvre through Cassino's northern end during the Third Battle for Cassino in mid-March 1944. Nazi snipers amid the ruins felled runners who carried messages, linesmen who attempted to lay telephone cable, and engineers who struggled to clear rubble. Supporting tanks of the New Zealand 19th Armoured Regiment were unable to follow the infantry, who were now forced to move over masonry debris and across 60-foot bomb craters. Amid this chaos of battle, the New Zealand attack became disorganised and faltered, with only isolated successes. (*NARA*)

(**Opposite, above**) A pair of Canadian 6-pounder anti-tank guns, one towed by a Universal Carrier (*left*), on either side of a narrow road at the entrance to the Liri Valley. Following behind were two self-propelled M7 'Priest' 105mm Gun Motor Carriage (GMC) vehicles, which are crossing the Gari River, a few miles to the south of Cassino near Sant' Apollinare, where it joins the Liri River as tributaries of the Garigliano River. The M7 105mm GMC became the standard self-propelled Howitzer in the Allied arsenal. (*NARA*)

(**Opposite, below**) After the Battle for Orsogna on the Adriatic coast, which lasted from the end of November 1943 until the beginning of January 1944, the 2nd New Zealand Division moved west across the Apennines to the Cassino sector. Here, situated along the bank of the Rapido River, infantrymen of the 28th Maori Battalion of the 2nd New Zealand Division watch for German movements during the massive Allied aerial bombardment of the Benedictine abbey atop Monte Cassino on 15 February 1944. Blockbuster bombs from over 250 Allied heavy and medium bombers turned the monastery into a pile of rubble that was to be utilised expertly by Nazi defenders for the next three months. The Maoris attacked on the night of 17 February and occupied the railway station and a hillock called the Hummocks, both south of the town of Cassino. The Germans counter-attacked the next day and the unsupported Maoris were compelled to retreat to their attack's start line. (*USAMHI*)

(**Opposite, above**) A New Zealand sniper takes aim at a Nazi target in the ruined town of Cassino well after the failed Third Battle for Cassino. Snipers were commonly employed on both sides. The massive aerial bombardment and artillery shelling of the town prior to the Third Battle in mid-March turned a locale that had an occasional intact structure into a single pile of rubble that was perfect for concealment. (*NARA*)

(**Above**) Wounded New Zealand infantrymen are evacuated by medical aides under a Red Cross flag amid the ruins of the town of Cassino, at the foot of Castle Hill, during the Third Battle for Cassino launched on 15 March 1944. (*NARA*)

(**Opposite, below**) Infantrymen of the French Expeditionary Corps (FEC), wearing their characteristic Adrian helmets, at a Browning 0.30-inch calibre light machine-gun outpost. The soldier (*right*) holds a Thompson 0.45-inch calibre submachine-gun demonstrating mostly American weapons among the FEC troops. (*NARA*)

(**Opposite**) In early February 1944, after the First Battle for Cassino ended in a lost Allied opportunity, two Moroccan *Goumiers* of the French Expeditionary Corps (FEC) north of the town adjust their kit over their traditionally striped woollen coats, *djellaba*. The term *Goum* referred to a company of armed North African mounted tribesmen who were employed during the French occupation of Morocco from 1908. The soldier on the left is wearing the French Army's characteristic Adrian helmet, while the one on the right has a Brodie pattern British steel helmet and is seen shouldering an antiquated bolt-action rifle. (*NARA*)

(**Above**) A French Expeditionary Corps (FEC) muleteer adjusts the heavy load of supplies on his charge in the rugged mountains north of Cassino. Moroccans and Algerians from the FEC had been successful in seizing some heights north of the town on the far bank of the Rapido River during the First Battle for Cassino from late January to early February 1944, and were to again demonstrate their skill and agility in mountain warfare during the opening days of Operation Diadem in mid-May. (*USAMHI*)

(**Opposite**) A wounded infantryman from the 3rd Algerian Division of the French Expeditionary Corps (FEC) leans against a tree with his head bandaged near Ausonia in the foothills of the Aurunci Mountains in mid-May 1944. The FEC, now comprising the French 1st Motorised, the Moroccan 2nd Infantry, the Moroccan 4th Mountain and the Algerian 3rd Infantry Divisions, had been re-deployed from the north of Cassino to the former British X Corps sector along the Garigliano River. There, the FEC cracked the Gustav Line, enabling the US II Corps' 85th and 88th Infantry Divisions, on its left flank, to continue its stalled attack along the Tyrrhenian coast. (*NARA*)

(**Above**) Two South African sappers exhibit a captured Nazi flag in the town of Cassino after the final Fourth Battle for Cassino after the British XIII Corps pierced the Gustav Line to the south of the town, necessitating the German withdrawal on 17 May 1944. (*NARA*)

(**Above**) After the German withdrawal from Cassino on 17 May 1944, South African sappers remove road debris following five months of bombardment. An M4 tank is situated to the left while Castle Hill, which housed enemy weapons in caves and pillboxes looms above in the background. (*NARA*)

(**Opposite, above**) South African infantrymen guard a group of German prisoners near an Italian road sign. On the road nearby, a heavily camouflaged M4 medium tank of the South African 6th Armoured Division in pursuit of retreating Germans in early June 1944. (*NARA*)

(**Opposite, above**) South African Basuto Pioneers with New Zealanders after unloading munitions from trucks for the combat along the Cassino sector in early 1944. The government of South Africa, due to its race policies, did not arm its tribesmen. Instead, a Native Military Corps was formed to be manned by black South Africans for pioneer, motor, labour and guard duties. (*NARA*)

Mortarmen from the Polish II Corps ready their 2-inch mortar next to a destroyed Nazi self-propelled gun in late February 1944. The Polish II Corps, comprising the 3rd Carpathian Rifles and 5th Kresowa Infantry Divisions, as well as the 2nd Armoured Brigade, were involved in the savage combat to capture the Benedictine abbey atop Monte Cassino during the final Fourth Battle for Cassino in mid-May 1944. (*NARA*)

(**Opposite, above**) Polish soldiers man positions upon an Italian mountain on 8 February 1944. The over-two-year odyssey of these Polish soldiers who fought in Italy spanned three continents, starting with Soviet captivity to the east of Moscow into the south-eastern Central Asian republics. From there the Poles continued trekking through Persia and Iraq into the British-controlled Middle East, where they were designated as Polish II Corps under General Wladyslaw Anders. Re-equipped by the British, they departed from Egypt for Italy's Adriatic coast and then to the Cassino sector. (*NARA*)

(**Opposite, below**) Polish II Corps soldiers from the 2nd Brigade of the 3rd Carpathian Rifles Division carry a dead comrade from the war-ravaged heights of Monte Cassino to the rear on 18 May 1944. To the left of the Polish infantrymen are dead German defenders of the town and monastery, who fought with extreme tenacity from well-prepared and concealed entrenchments that provided a tactical advantage of firing down on the Poles climbing uphill from crag to crag with their weapons and ammunition. The Poles incurred thousands of casualties to take the heights by 18 May 1944 as the Germans had withdrawn the night before. (*NARA*)

(**Opposite, above**) Jews from the Palestine Mandate fought in Eighth Army across North Africa. During the Italian Campaign, there was one independent brigade within the Eighth Army participating in the combat. Infantrymen from the brigade ride a Churchill tank towards the frontlines. (*Author's Collection*)

(**Above**) Ernie Pyle, the famous Pulitzer Prize-winning Scripps-Howard War Correspondent (*seated, front row, second from right*) talks with American crewmen of the 191st Tank Battalion at Anzio. Pyle's travels as a journalist were ubiquitous producing flattering press releases of ordinary American soldiers fighting on the different fronts. He was felled by a Japanese sniper's bullet on 18 April 1945 on Okinawa. (*USAMHI*)

(**Opposite, below**) An Italian 105mm gun crew from an artillery regiment in the 1st Motorised Group fires their weapon in the mountainous area near Cerro Grasso on 7 March 1944. As is evident by the large wooden wheels, this was one of the antiquated pieces of ordnance used by the Italians prior to joining the Allied cause after Italy's capitulation in September 1943. (*USAMHI*)

(**Left**) Field-Marshal Albert Kesselring, a pioneer and visionary *Luftwaffe* officer, was appointed commander-in-chief, south, in December 1941 with his headquarters based near Rome. He commanded Hitler's air squadrons in the MTO and reported to the Italian Fascist leader Benito Mussolini as well. Having combat experience in both Poland and France, he was instrumental in the development of tactical aerial assault, notably with his squadrons of Ju 87 or *Stuka* dive bombers in 1939 and 1940, which he brought to the MTO along the North African littoral. During the Sicily Campaign, Kesselring retained tactical authority over all German military units in southern Italy, even though he was a *Luftwaffe* rather than an army officer. At odds with the other German field-marshal in northern Italy, Erwin Rommel, Kesselring advocated a tenacious defence of southern Italy and the building of defensive fortification belts across the peninsula's rugged mountainous and rivers. With Rommel's transfer to northern France, Hitler accepted Kesselring's counter-attacking strategy to repel an Allied invasion of the Italian mainland at Salerno, which ultimately failed. Forced onto the defensive, Kesselring utilised a harsh winter climate, interior lines and mountain redoubts as Nazi 'force multipliers' with his manpower deficiencies. (*NARA*)

(**Right**) German General Heinrich von Vietinghoff, a First World War veteran, served as commanding general of the Nazi's Tenth Army in southern Italy. Prior to his leadership role in Italy, he commanded a Panzer division and corps in France and Russia, respectively, and served as the German Fifth Army commander in France prior to Operation Husky in July 1943. After the Allied invasion of Sicily, he was dispatched to Italy to command the Tenth Army based on his aggressive Panzer tactical reputation from Russia. Vietinghoff contested the Salerno landings with fierce armoured counter-attacks by Generals Hans Hube's XIV and Traugott Herr's LXXVI Panzer Corps that severely threatened the Fifth Army beachhead within days of the landings in September. After his losses there, he was forced onto the defensive along the sequential defensive lines erected. (*Author's Collection*)

(**Left**) The German Fourteenth Army, a new formation, was commanded by General Eberhard von Mackensen, a Prussian aristocrat like Vietinghoff. Mackensen's father had been a field-marshal and the younger one earned a reputation as a rugged Panzer leader in Russia while in command of a Panzer corps there and later the 1st *Panzer-armee*. Mackensen's Fourteenth Army was charged with the organisation of the defence of the Anzio sector after the successful Operation Shingle landings on 22 January 1944. The Nazi aim was initially to block any Allied advance to the Alban Hills. After successfully completing this task, Mackensen directed his forces to destroy Lucas's VI Corps at their beachhead via counter-attacks launched beginning on the night of 3–4 February aimed at Campoleone, then The Factory at Aprilia and finally the Anzio–Nettuno beaches. Like his initial adversary, Lucas, he too was sacked after the Allied break-out from Anzio. (*Author's Collection*)

(**Right**) Lieutenant-General Fridolin von Senger und Etterlin took over the command of German XIV Corps from Hube in late autumn 1943, in time for the intense mountain conflicts culminating in the First Battle of Cassino. Intriguingly, Senger und Etterlin, an Oxford-educated officer, had strong roots in Catholicism as well as being a lay Benedictine, which was pertinent as he was to command the defences involved at the abbey at Monte Cassino. A First World War veteran field artilleryman and a post-war Weimar cavalryman, Senger und Etterlin commanded a brigade during the French *Blitzkrieg* in 1940 and led the 17th Panzer Division during the Russian winter campaign of 1942. On Sicily, he served as a liaison with the Italian military commanders there and was shocked by the incomplete and disorganised defences. (*NARA*)

General Traugott Herr, commander of the German LXXVI Panzer Corps, was highly successful at disengaging his 29th Panzer Grenadier and 26th Panzer Divisions from the British Eighth Army's slow advance and deliver them to the Salerno battlefield, where he was instrumental in orchestrating the Nazi counter-attack of 13 September 1943 that almost compelled Clark to evacuate the US VI Corps from the southern half of the beachhead to the south of the Sele River. At Anzio, Herr was to also command the LXXVI Panzer Corps, comprising a number of units fed into the cauldron there. In mid-February 1945, Herr was promoted to command the Wehrmacht's Tenth Army when Vietinghoff replaced Kesselring upon the latter's appointment to commander-in-chief, west. (*Author's Collection*)

Three German paratroopers in the Anzio sector scanning for Allied movement. These elite soldiers from the 4th Parachute Division were situated behind the Moletta River between the Tyrrhenian Sea and Carroceto. The parachutists were seated next to their MG 34 light machine-gun and wore camouflaged jump smocks with a *Luftwaffe* eagle displayed on the standard *Fallschirmjäger* helmet (*right parachutist*) covered with netting. (*Author's Collection*)

As prisoners-of-war, these German parachutists march past their Allied captors at Cassino in a well-ordered formation in their customary camouflaged jump smocks. The elite parachutists, who tenaciously defended the ruins of the Benedictine abbey upon Monte Cassino and within the town below the heights, were from the 1st Parachute Division, commanded by Major-General Richard Heidrich. The division comprised three rifle regiments and a machine-gun battalion at the Cassino sector. (NARA)

German officers of the 955th Regiment that had defended Cisterna are escorted to the rear by an American infantryman carrying an M1 carbine. The Nazi officers carry briefcases with some of their belongings for their stay in prisoner stockades. (USAMHI)

German youths were among many of the Nazis that surrendered to infantrymen of the US 3rd Division at Cisterna in late May after the Anzio break-out. These soldiers from the *Wehrmacht* 114th Jäger Division had been guarding against an Allied amphibious landing on the Adriatic Sea as well as fighting Italian partisans in northern Italy, before hastily being deployed to seal the Allied bridgehead at Anzio. Many of the divisional units in the Fourteenth Army were reconstituted to combat strength from a variety of German manpower pools, including young teenagers. (*USAMHI*)

During the third week of April 1944, a British officer at Anzio interrogates a young German, who was captured from a beached one-man midget submarine, called a *Neger*, intended to disrupt the Allied invasion fleet offshore that was building up VI Corps for a renewed offensive out of the besieged bridgehead. The German craft was a hollowed torpedo shell fitted with a new cockpit and controls section for the sole occupant. A conventional torpedo was slung beneath the manned torpedo. (*USAMHI*)

At Anzio, a young dead bespectacled German *panzergrenadier* lies in the mud after a failed attack against Allied lines. German reinforcements at Anzio were drawn from a number of different quarters, including the German home front, and Mackensen's Fourteenth Army formations were in a constant state of re-shuffling, but fought with courage and determination, regardless of their young age, at Anzio. (*USAMHI*)

Chapter Four

Operation Shingle and the German Encirclement at Anzio

Fifth Army's VI Corps unopposed assault at Anzio, Operation Shingle, on 22 January 1944 simultaneously occurred with the failure of US II Corps and British X Corps to breach the Gustav Line. Clark intended that his winter offensive along the Gustav Line would draw Kesselring's reserves away from VI Corps landings at Anzio, enabling Lucas's assaulting Allied forces to rapidly push past the Alban Hills and on to Rome, just over 30 miles from the beachhead. Clark's other strategic aim was based on piercing the Gustav Line at Cassino and then entering the Liri Valley for his Fifth Army's advance towards Rome along Highway 6. In the British Eighth Army sector on Italy's Adriatic coast, Leese's divisions were to attack from Ortona towards Pescara on the Rome Line.

For Winston Churchill, the amphibious assault at Anzio, 70 miles north-west of the Gustav Line at Cassino, was to be a *coup de main* end-run around the stalemated conflict along the Gustav Line, providing a more expeditious approach to capture Rome. Despite the opposition and pessimism of some of the Allied generals involved, the successful landing took the Germans by complete surprise. However, the near loss at Salerno had instilled an air of caution in the top American commanders at Anzio. Clark told Lucas, 'not to stick your neck out, like I did at Salerno.' As a result of this collegial advice, Lucas's initial amphibious success became a cautious probe towards Rome instead of a rapid thrust past the Alban Hills.

The Allied armada of over 240 vessels, which emanated from the Bay of Naples on 21 January, after an inauspicious invasion rehearsal on 19 January at Pozzuoli when many infantry and artillery laden DUKWs had inadvertently sunk, encountered calm seas. The invasion fleet appeared off Anzio at 0200hrs on 22 January and lowered landing craft. A brief rocket barrage was unleashed on the port of Anzio. Clark anticipated strong German resistance at the Shingle beachheads, as was experienced at Salerno. However, almost complete surprise was achieved as Nazi forces were not defending the beaches or the towns of Anzio and Nettuno. Sporadic long-range enemy shelling from the Alban Hills did little harm. The town of Anzio had been essentially evacuated and the Allies concluded their *coup de main* assault a success.

Without any significant ground opposition by the Germans, Lucas landed 36,000 men with a seven-day ration of supplies along with over 3,000 vehicles. The British 1st Infantry Division, under Major-General William R.C. Penney, two units of RM Commandos (Nos. 9 and 43), and the 46th Royal Tank Regiment (RTR) were to land north of Anzio Town at Red, Yellow and Green beaches in the Task Force Peter zone. The American landing zone sectors, at Task Force X-Ray's Red and Green beaches south of Nettuno, were assaulted by the US 3rd Infantry Division, while Task Force 81 unloaded the US 504th PIR and 508th Parachute Infantry Battalion of the 82nd Airborne Division, three US Ranger battalions, and the 751st Tank Battalion to occupy both Anzio and Nettuno. Just inland from Anzio were the Padiglione Woods, which would house Allied artillery positions and supply dumps. Within forty-eight hours, a beachhead of 7 miles deep and 16 miles wide was established. Lucas wanted his assault waves to immediately go on the defensive until reinforcements, to augment his force to 50,000 troops, as well as fifteen and ten days' further allotments of supplies and ammunition, respectively, were landed.

Both Clark and Lucas's tentative tactics for Operation Shingle enabled Kesselring to redeploy the German Fourteenth Army under General Eberhard von Mackensen, to meet this latest Allied threat on the pathway to Rome. Initially, 40,000 Nazi troops under Mackensen arrived. At 0500hrs on 22 January, Kesselring began mobilising all of his available infantry and artillery from as far north as Genoa, Rimini, and Leghorn to add to the Nazi containment force of the Anzio–Nettuno beachhead. Additional German reinforcements were summoned from southern France and the Balkans, as well as those stationed against Leese's Eighth Army on the Adriatic Front.

By the end of Shingle's D-Day, Kesselring deduced that the Allies were not going to push far inland, despite the road to Rome being open. Railways and trucks brought German units to the Anzio battlefield sooner than the Allies thought feasible. Elements of the German 3rd Panzer Grenadier and Hermann Göring Divisions, which days before were sent to Vietinghoff's Tenth Army fortifications along the Garigliano River, were now re-deployed to the Anzio beachhead. Other German reinforcements from the 29th Panzer Grenadier and the 71st Infantry Divisions arrived as early as D-Day. On 26 January, lead elements of the 65th and 362nd Infantry Divisions arrived from their northern Italy garrison locations. General von Mackensen had elements of eight divisions ringing the Anzio beachhead to contain any Allied expansion. Additionally, Kesselring had major elements of five more divisions in transit to the area. Although some Allied reinforcements, such as part of the US 1st Armoured and the 45th Infantry Divisions, were soon to disembark from VI Corps reserve, Kesselring positioned elements of eight Nazi divisions against roughly four Allied ones.

On 24 January, Lucas sent out reconnaissance patrols to gauge enemy strength on roads towards Campoleone and Cisterna, the front's forward flanks. The British 24th Guards Brigade, after having moved approximately 4 miles from positions in

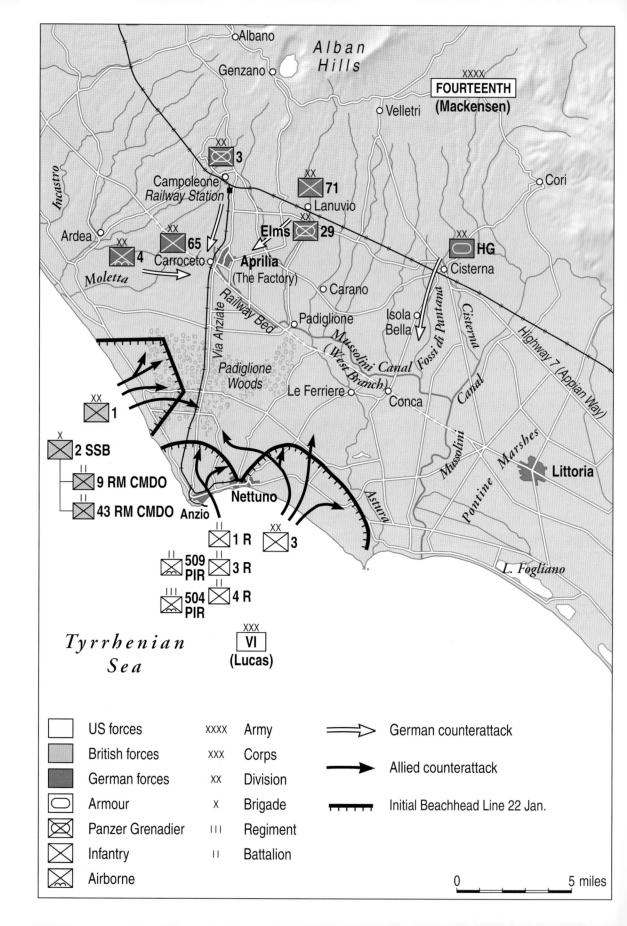

Albano

Genzano

Alban Hills

XXXX
FOURTEENTH
(Mackensen)

Velletri

Cori

XX
3

Campoleone
Railway Station

XX
71

Lanuvio

Ardea

XX
4

XX
65

Carroceto

Elms

XX
29

XX
HG

Cisterna

Aprilia
(The Factory)

Moletta

Carano

XX

Incastro

Railway Bed

Via Anziate

*Padiglione
Woods*

Padiglione

Isola
Bella

Cisterna

Fossi di Pantana

*Mussolini Canal
(West Branch)*

Le Ferriere

Conca

Mussolini Canal

Highway 7 (Appian Way)

Pontine Marshes

Littoria

XX
1

X
2 SSB

II
9 RM CMDO

II
43 RM CMDO

Nettuno

Anzio

Astura

L. Fogliano

II
1 R

XX
3

II
**509
PIR**

II
3 R

III
**504
PIR**

II
4 R

XXX
VI
(Lucas)

*Tyrrhenian
Sea*

☐	US forces	XXXX	Army	⟹ German counterattack
▨	British forces	XXX	Corps	➡ Allied counterattack
▰	German forces	XX	Division	
⬭	Armour	X	Brigade	┳━ Initial Beachhead Line 22 Jan.
⊠	Panzer Grenadier	III	Regiment	
☒	Infantry	II	Battalion	
⊠	Airborne			

0   5 miles

the Padiglione Woods toward Campoleone, came under intense fire at the village of Carroceto. Also, British infantry from the 3rd Brigade was precariously extended and visible along the road to Campoleone. Regiments in this brigade, such as the Sherwood Foresters, suffered grievously with many officers killed.

American units on the right flank, moving north along the road to Cisterna, met elements of the Hermann Göring Division entrenched in fortified farmhouses from which these Nazi veteran troops resisted a further advance. Nazi shelling from remote locales, coupled with *Luftwaffe* air-raids on the beachhead, lent credence to the Allied suspicions that the Germans had reacted strongly. Also, rough seas erupted creating some havoc along the beaches among the landing craft.

A disaster for the Allies occurred on 29–30 January. A force of 767 US Rangers from the 1st and 3rd Battalions moved towards Cisterna along an irrigation canal, the Fossi di Pantana (Pantano Ditch), which was a partially dry extension of the Mussolini Canal. The Fossi di Pantana provided cover for the rangers to get within 1.5 miles of Cisterna without detection. As the rangers emerged from the ditch into open terrain to the outskirts of the town, elements of the Hermann Göring Division ambushed them with over 450 rangers compelled to surrender. Only a handful of the attacking American elite force returned from this assault. This ranger movement was intended to confuse the Germans about the main US 15th Infantry Regiment (3rd Division) and the 4th Ranger Battalion attack along the Isola Bella–Cisterna Road. However, this larger American infantry force was also stopped near Isola Bella, less than a mile from their objective and relief of their fellow rangers. Truscott's troops dug-in for what was soon to become a siege. Both Alexander and Clark decided that the beachhead was to shift to the defensive and prepare for a Nazi counter-attack, as had occurred at Salerno days after the landing there.

Operation Shingle: Landings by Allied VI Corps (Lucas), 22 January 1944 at Anzio–Nettuno. The British 1st Division and the attached 2nd Special Service Brigade (SSB) comprising No. 9 and No. 43 Royal Marine (RM) Commandos, landed unopposed north-west of Anzio, forming a perimeter paralleling the Moletta River and extending into the Padiglione Woods. Three US Army Ranger (R) battalions, along with the attached 504th Parachute Infantry Regiment and the 509th Parachute Infantry Battalion of the US 82nd Airborne Division, secured Anzio and Nettuno and established an initial perimeter a mile inland astride the Via Anziate. East of Nettuno, the US 3rd Division's three infantry regiments landed abreast, forming the VI Corps right flank. Elements of the US 7th Infantry Regiment met the RM Commandos near the Padiglione Woods, the 30th Infantry moved towards Le Ferriere, while the 15th Infantry on the far right assumed defensive positions paralleling the Astura River. The Allies dug-in concentrating their force over eight days as the Germans reacted quickly and contained the invaders forming the Fourteenth Army under Mackensen. This enemy army was initially comprised (from east to west) of elements of the Hermann Göring Division, near Cisterna, the 71st Infantry Division, in the vicinity of Lanuvio, the 3rd Panzer Grenadier Division, near Campoleone, the 65th Infantry Division, situated between Ardea and Campoleone, and the 4th Parachute Division, located north of the Moletta River. (*Philip Schwartzberg, Meridian Mapping, Minneapolis, MN*)

Although the Germans too had suffered casualties, their Fourteenth Army contingents contained the beachhead. By 30 January, the Allied defensive perimeter extended to the mouth of the Moletta River on the sea coast, to the north of the Mussolini Canal above the Pontine Marshes and Padiglione Woods in the centre, and only on the flanks towards Cisterna and Campoleone to the south of the railway line.

It has been debated that if the Allies had pushed more rapidly inland on 22–23 January 1944 to quickly get beyond the Alban Hills, Rome could have been reached, thereby compelling the Nazis to abandon the Gustav Line. In fact, a reconnaissance Jeep patrol from the US 3rd Division did reach the outskirts of Rome on the morning of 22 January without meeting any Nazi forces.

Churchill quipped about VI Corps' missed opportunity: 'I had hoped that we would be hurling a wildcat ashore, but all we got was a stranded whale.'

Alternatively, as British 1st Division commanding general Penney noted about a premature Allied move into the Alban Hills shortly after landing, 'we would have one day in Rome and eighteen months in prisoner-of-war camps.' Another stalemate in the Italian Campaign had developed at Anzio.

US 3rd Division infantrymen wade ashore from Landing Craft Infantry (LCI) transports during Operation Shingle on 22 January 1944 at X-Ray Beach, 4 miles to the south of Anzio. Some DUKWs had already landed (*right*). Black smoke emanated from Allied ships struck by Nazi guns from the Alban Hills as escorting destroyers made smokescreens to shield Allied vessels from *Luftwaffe* aircraft. (*USAMHI*)

Two American infantrymen of the US
3rd Division wring out cloth wrappings after
their unopposed landing at the beachhead
south of Nettuno on 22 January 1944. In the
background are amphibious DUKWs, which
were instrumental in bringing both troops and
supplies from offshore transports during the
initial and subsequent phases of the operation.
(*NARA*)

Infantrymen from the British 1st Division
struggle in chest-high water at their landing
areas on 22 January 1944. The unfavourable
hydrographic gradient at the shallow, soft
British Task Force Peter beaches halted
landing operations there as British 1st Division
assault troops were transferred to the
crowded Anzio Harbour area. (*Author's Collection*)

(**Opposite, above**) Royal Navy ratings and British sappers secure heavy pontoons to assist landings and prevent disruption of reinforcement efforts in rough seas at the Operation Shingle beachhead a few days after the unopposed amphibious landings of 22 January 1944. Anzio and Nettuno Harbours were both captured intact and without enemy resistance. (*NARA*)

(**Opposite, below**) A panoramic view of the US 3rd Infantry Division's landing area at X-Ray Beach south of Anzio and Nettuno. A column of amphibious DUKWs (*foreground*) brings troops and supplies inland over some matting material, which provided traction in the soft sand. At the shoreline, Landing Ship Tanks (LSTs) with their hull doors open utilise pontoon bridges to enable their vehicular cargo to reach the sand. Other DUKWs and transports of the Allied armada are in the distance. (*USAMHI*)

(**Above**) A British-crewed DUKW brings supplies from the water right onto a beach at Nettuno. The great utility of these vehicles was derived from their ability to be loaded from transports offshore and then amphibiously moved to land where they were to become wheeled trucks for overland passage. (*USAMHI*)

(**Opposite, above**) British M4 medium tanks and infantry move out from the shallow beaches near Anzio. Accompanying the British 1st Infantry Division at the Task Force *Peter* beaches were the tanks of the 46th (Liverpool Welsh) Royal Tank Regiment (RTR). (*NARA*)

(**Opposite, below**) Royal Marine (RM) Commandos (*centre*) of Nos. 9 and 43 units within the British 2nd Special Service Brigade link up with US Rangers of the 6615th Ranger Force (Provisional) (*far left and right*), in the vicinity of the Via Anziate soon after the successful seizure of the town and port of Anzio on 22 January 1944. The RM units landed at Green beach in the Task Force Peter sector and pushed inland to the south-east edge of the Padiglione Woods. The Rangers, who had landed at 0200hrs on D-Day between Anzio and Nettuno, established a perimeter a mile inland from the port towns by mid-morning. (*NARA*)

(**Above**) American combat engineers probe the bank of an Anzio waterway with bayonets and wooden stakes to detect landmines. Detonation for some of these devices on the beach as well as in Anzio and Nettuno accounted for some of the 200 total casualties reported for the landings on 22 January 1944. (*USAMHI*)

(**Opposite, above**) A Landing Craft Infantry (LCI) partially sunk and afire on the morning of 22 January 1944. German Focke-Wulf 190 fighter-bombers raided the fleet on D-Day sinking the transport. The German Focke-Wulf 190 A-5 was developed in 1943 for ground-attack and anti-shipping with bombs and torpedoes. In all, about fifty enemy fighter-bomber sorties were mounted on D-Day against the beachhead with seven German and three Allied fighters shot down. (*USAMHI*)

(**Opposite, below**) A British Oerlikon 20mm anti-aircraft gun crew aboard an Allied vessel adds to the anti-aircraft fire that appears as black bursts in the sky. On D-Day + 1, the *Luftwaffe* launched more damaging attacks against the Allied shipping in Anzio Harbour. Nazi dive-bombers attacked with bombs, aerial torpedoes, and the radio-controlled armour-piercing glider bombs that were effective on the Allied armada at Salerno. On this day, HMS *Janus*, a destroyer, was sunk. (*USAMHI*)

(**Above**) As part of the anti-aircraft defences, American soldiers fill a barrage balloon. Balloons were tethered with metal cables, capable of destroying low-flying *Luftwaffe* aircraft upon collision, over the Allied beachhead and harbours. (*USAMHI*)

(**Above**) A combination of anti-aircraft (AA) defences at Anzio Harbour on 30 January 1944 with a 40mm Bofors AA gun and its crew (*foreground*). Aloft, a barrage balloon (*background*) is tethered to deter low-flying fighter aircraft from strafing and bombing the harbour. Aboard the Landing Ship Tank (LST) in the harbour with its bow ramps open for the unloading of cargo (*background right*) was its assortment of AA ordnance. Also, extensive smoke screens at Anzio were utilised. During the first week of the Anzio invasion, the *Luftwaffe* lost almost 100 planes. (*USAMHI*)

(**Opposite, above**) The excellent 90mm M1 anti-aircraft gun of A Battery, 216th AA Battalion of the US Coast Artillery within its sandbag-reinforced weapon pit at the Anzio beachhead. This weapon, which was a vital piece of defensive ordnance on American beachheads on all fronts, replaced the obsolescent 3-inch AA gun in 1938. (*NARA*)

(**Opposite, below**) Two American-crewed Spitfire Mk IX aircraft of the US 307th Fighter Squadron at its base at Nettuno in the initial days of February 1944, to provide immediate fighter support for the beachhead. This temporary airfield had to be evacuated by the middle of the month due to frequent Nazi artillery-fire from the Alban Hills. (*USAMHI*)

(**Above**) An M10 Gun-Mounted Carriage (GMC) of a Tank Destroyer battalion moves along a ruined section of Anzio. Buildings and roadways destroyed by Nazi aerial and artillery bombardment and the barrage balloon aloft (*background*) served as evidence of the four-month siege. (*USAMHI*)

(**Opposite, above**) An area of Nettuno under intense German long-range heavy artillery bombardment, with a hotel struck by an explosive shell. The near continuous aerial and artillery assault necessitated a variety of tactical adaptations on the part of the Allies within the Anzio–Nettuno perimeter from late January to mid-May 1944. (*USAMHI*)

(**Opposite, below**) The Allies situated a variety of field guns within the Anzio–Nettuno perimeter to provide effective counter-battery fire against German artillery targets as well as enemy troop and armour concentrations. Here, a British Breech-Loading (BL) 4.5-inch Medium gun from the Royal Artillery's Scottish Horse, a Yeomanry regiment of the Territorial Army, is in its weapon pit readying for firing. This ordnance was capable of hurling a 55lb high-explosive (HE) shell 21,000 yards and had nothing in common with the Quick-Firing (QF) 4.5-inch Howitzer or 4.5-inch anti-aircraft guns. (*NARA*)

(**Opposite, above**) A British soldier next to an inflated rubber 'dummy' tank intended to confuse Nazi artillery and aerial spotters located near the Alban Hills, which provided an excellent observation point of the Allied beach-head. The British had extensive experience implementing deception methods that masked troop deployments and created notional formations to confuse the enemy about the Allied Order of Battle. Dudley Clarke and Jasper Maskelyne were two prominent British officers who excelled at such masquerade and camouflage techniques throughout the entire war. (*USAMHI*)

(**Above**) The underground headquarters of US VI Corps in Nettuno. Telephone switchboards, radio communications and maps-rooms were located below street level to provide a modicum of safety from the Nazi bombardment of the town. (*USAMHI*)

(**Opposite, below**) Elements of the 2nd Battalion of the 504th Parachute Infantry Regiment (PIR) dig-in near the Mussolini Canal, which constituted the extreme right of the Allied perimeter south of Anzio and Nettuno abutting the Pontine Marshes. The paratrooper on the right carries a smoke generator to mask the eventual crossing of this man-made barrier at the end of January 1944. (*NARA*)

(**Opposite, above**) Two American infantrymen from a 3rd Division 60mm mortar crew cover their ears while firing their round from the shelter of a sandbag-lined weapon pit near an embankment within the contained Anzio beachhead soon after the successful Shingle landing operations. Infantry support weapons such as this mortar were to prove critical in the defence of the Allied perimeter at Anzio–Nettuno once the Nazi Fourteenth Army counter-attack commenced during the early days of February 1944. (*USAMHI*)

(**Above**) Allied soldiers attempted to find protective cover wherever possible. Here, two American tank crewmen clean a 0.30-inch calibre Browning light machine-gun under the cover of a masonry lean-to next to their M4 medium tank. (*USAMHI*)

(**Opposite, below**) German prisoners-of-war are escorted to the Allied rear echelon in the Carroceto area north of Anzio along the Via Anziate on 19 February 1944. Note the numerous American infantrymen's protective foxholes at the side of the roadway. Carroceto was heavily contested by the British with the support of a battalion of the 504th Parachute Infantry Regiment (PIR) in reserve. The Nazi 65th and 715th Motorised Infantry Divisions along with the 3rd Panzer Grenadier Division made numerous counter-attacks against this Allied salient north of Anzio. (*USAMHI*)

(**Opposite, above**) British infantrymen from the Irish Guards of the 24th Guards Brigade, 1st British Division advance along the Via Anziate behind an M4 medium tank of the 46th (Liverpool Welsh) Royal Tank Regiment in their movement north from their landing beaches towards the 'First Overpass', the Carroceto railway station, and Aprilia (The Factory). This unit, among other British infantry formations, suffered heavy casualties and was forced to withdraw from the salient, 'The Thumb', which extended towards the Campoleone Station, once the German Fourteenth Army counter-attack commenced on 3 February 1944. (*NARA*)

(**Opposite, below**) US Rangers who were captured near Cisterna by elements of the Hermann Göring Division when they exited from an irrigation ditch, the Fossi di Pantana, on 30 January 1944 are paraded through Rome as Nazi propaganda trophies in early February 1944 before going into prisoner-of-war camps. The ruins of the Roman Coliseum (*background*) are visible. (*Author's Collection*)

(**Above**) Dead Nazi soldiers lie in an irrigation ditch after attempting to infiltrate and sever the US 45th Infantry Division's lines of communication in early March 1944. The 'Thunderbirds', now under the command of Major-General William W. Eagles (replacing the ailing Major-General Troy Middleton), along with elements of the US 1st Armoured Division, were reserve formations that did not participate in the 22 January amphibious landings. (*USAMHI*)

(**Opposite, above**) A destroyed German tank near Cisterna after the main Nazi counter-attacks were launched in early February 1944. Field-Marshal Kesselring requested *Wehrmacht* formations to be transferred to Anzio from northern Italy, southern Italy, Germany, France and Yugoslavia. With this rapid German build-up in the Anzio–Nettuno area, Kesselring ordered the Fourteenth Army headquarters, under General Eberhard von Mackensen, to assume operational control of the battlefield on 25 January. (*USAMHI*)

(**Opposite, below**) Two M4 medium tanks of the 46th (Liverpool Welsh) Royal Tank Regiment (RTR) advance inland from the Allied beachhead to support the British 1st Division from the Nazi counter-attack during the first week of February 1944. (*NARA*)

(**Above**) British 1st Infantry Division troops pass through some of the ruins of Anzio behind a towed 40mm Bofors anti-aircraft gun in mid-February 1944. These veteran infantrymen were moving north of Anzio in an attempt to staunch Nazi counter-attacks from the amassed Fourteenth Army divisions that had ringed the VI Corps perimeter, notably along the Via Anziate between the Padiglione Woods and Carroceto. (*NARA*)

An American soldier attaches anti-personnel mines to barbed wire to secure the 3rd Division's perimeter from Nazi infiltration south of Nettuno. In addition to the barbed wire and landmines, 3rd Division infantrymen on 22–23 January 1944 seized and destroyed bridges over the Mussolini Canal to deny the enemy a roadway across the barrier, which was 240 feet wide from one embankment to the other with waters 10–20 feet deep. (NARA)

Dead German paratroopers sprawled across barbed wire on which they became entangled as they attempted to penetrate the Allied perimeter near the Moletta River, which comprised the north-western end of the British 1st Division's defensive sector. (USAMHI)

Chapter Five

Cassino's Second, Third and Fourth Battles and the Breakthrough at the Gustav Line

Second Battle for Cassino

After two failed US II Corps assaults to break through the Gustav Line north and south of Cassino, Clark was to deploy Eighth Army divisions to follow-up on the ground gained by Ryder's US 34th Infantry Division's three attacking regiments and the attached 142nd Infantry from the 36th Division. The 2nd New Zealand Division was brought west across the Apennines on 30 January. However, amid controversy, it was not committed to support the US II Corps attack north of the town and monastery. Tuker's 4th Indian Division had been sent by Leese in early February 1944 and, upon joining the 2nd New Zealand Division, Freyberg was to command them as II New Zealand Corps. The American infantrymen were exhausted from the terrain, harsh winter weather and the gruesome combat of the First Battle for Cassino. American lines in the vicinity of Snakeshead Ridge, north-west of the abbey, and to the north of the town, were held by the remnants of these four American infantry regiments that started the first assault at Cassino at the end of January 1944, now each battle-depleted to one-tenth of their original strength.

The Second Battle of Cassino, Operation Avenger, from 15–17 February 1944, began with a massive four-hour morning air-raid on the Benedictine abbey by Allied medium and heavy bombers, followed by artillery bombardment. Both Tuker and Freyberg convinced the Allied chain of command, Clark, Alexander and Wilson, that the monastery's obliteration was a prerequisite for a successful attack as the Germans were overlooking their moves from within the abbey.

German XIV Corps commanding general Senger und Etterlin forbade the abbey's use, except for those wounded, and positioned his troops on the nearby slopes of Monte Cassino beneath the towering edifice. Only the monastery's outer walls were destroyed from the bombardment of 15 February, while the west wing and cellars

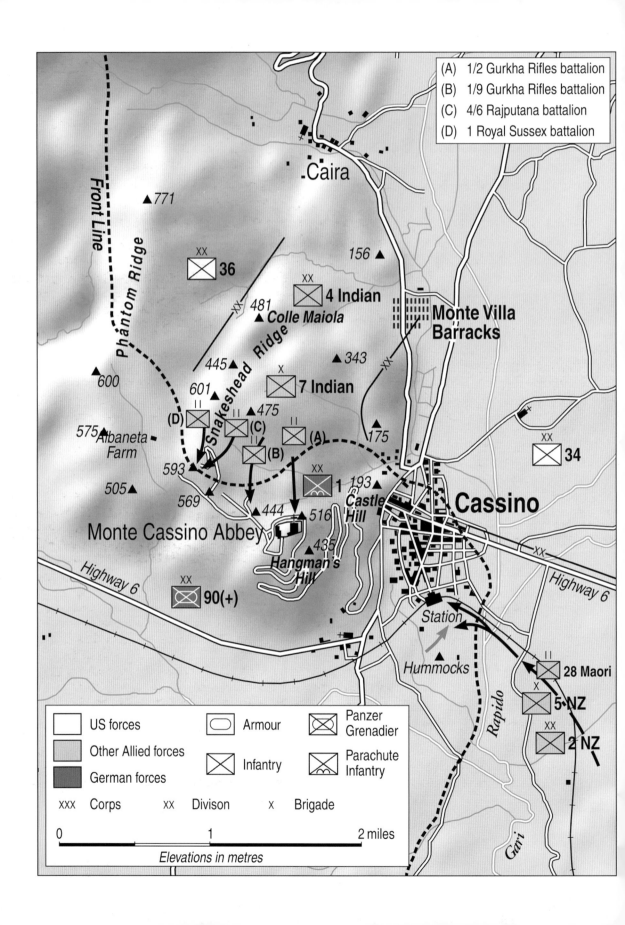

(A) 1/2 Gurkha Rifles battalion
(B) 1/9 Gurkha Rifles battalion
(C) 4/6 Rajputana battalion
(D) 1 Royal Sussex battalion

Caira

▲ 771

156 ▲

Monte Villa
Barracks

XX 36

XX 4 Indian

XX 481
▲ *Colle Maiola*

Snakeshead Ridge

445 ▲

▲ 343

▲ 600

601 ▲

X 7 Indian

175 ▲

(D) ‖

(C) ‖ ▲ 475

(A) ‖

575 ▲
*Albaneta
Farm*

(B) ‖

593 ▲

505 ▲

569 ▲

▲ 444

XX 1

193 ▲
*Castle
Hill*

Cassino

XX 34

Monte Cassino Abbey

516 ▲

▲ 435
*Hangman's
Hill*

Highway 6

XX 90(+)

Station

Highway 6

Hummocks ▲

‖ 28 Maori

Rapido

X 5 NZ

XX 2 NZ

Gari

US forces		Armour		Panzer Grenadier
Other Allied forces		Infantry		Parachute Infantry
German forces				

xxx Corps   xx Divison   x Brigade

0   1   2 miles

Elevations in metres

remained intact. The Germans transformed the ruins into a defensive bastion after dark. Advanced units of the 4th Indian Division's 7th Brigade, receiving little warning of the aerial assault, incurred some friendly-fire casualties.

Freyberg's plan was a continuation of Cassino's first battle and he gave it only a fifty percent chance of success. Its scope was extremely small in terms of the sizes of the forces deployed. The combat veterans of the 4th Indian Division were to attack in battalion-strength southwards past the American positions, which they relieved on 12 February, to seize Points 593, 569, 444 and 516 (in metres) as a prelude to capture the monastery and then advance down the hill and cut the road to the town of Cassino. The 28th Maori Battalion of the battle-hardened 2nd New Zealand Division was to separately cross the Rapido River in the vicinity of the town's railway station, 1 mile south of the Cassino, to ultimately rendezvous with the anticipated victorious Indians, thereby, gaining an entry into the Liri Valley via Highway 6.

Two separate attacks by the 7th Indian Brigade's 1st Battalion Royal Sussex Regiment and the 4/6th Rajputana Rifles failed to capture Point 593 on 15–16 February

---

The Second Battle for Cassino. The 4th Indian Division relieved the US 34th and 36th Divisions' regiments on 12 February 1944. Four 7th Indian Brigade battalions attacked through the Americans' gained ground in the mountains along the 'elbow-shaped' Snakeshead Ridge north-west of the monastery. On the night of 15 February, a company of the 1st Royal Sussex probed German forward slopes of Point 593 at the southern bend of Snakeshead Ridge, 1,000 yards from the monastery. Point 593 had to be seized before Point 444, at the ridge's eastern end, was attacked to prevent enfilading fire. Half of the attacking three platoons became casualties just 50 yards from their start-line. At 2300hrs on 16 February, an additional 360 of the 1st/Royal Sussex unsuccessfully attacked amid friendly artillery-fire, Nazi grenade attack machine-gunfire, and hand-to-hand combat. In two nights, twelve of fifteen officers and 162 of 313 men were lost. At 2400hrs on 17 February, the 4/6th Rajputana Rifles re-stormed Point 593, losing 200 officers and other ranks within two hours. At 0200hrs on 18 February, the 1/9th and the 1/2nd Gurkha Rifles, starting further east, directly attacked Point 444 and Monastery Hill (Point 516), respectively. The 1/9th Gurkhas came under enfilading fire from Point 593, losing 100 men. The 1/2nd Gurkhas were felled by German parachutists' grenades along Monastery Hill's northern slope, channelling them into a Nazi minefield, killing half of the leading platoons with enemy machine-guns raking the survivors. The 1/2nd Gurkhas made it to 400 yards of the monastery, losing a dozen officers and 140 other ranks. The four Indian battalions incurred almost 650 casualties with the Nazis retaining the heights. On the night of 17 February, only two companies of the 28th (Maori) Battalion of the 2nd New Zealand Division's 5th Brigade crossed the Rapido-flooded terrain from the east along a narrow railway causeway that sappers repaired under Nazi gunfire, limiting the attack's size. The Maoris captured Cassino's railway station. However, the decimation of the Indian battalions nullified the planned rendezvous to force entry into the Liri Valley via Highway 6. Despite a masking smokescreen to protect the sappers from German gunfire while erecting other Bailey bridges for Allied armour and anti-tank guns, the construction was prevented by Nazi shelling, which idled over 180 tanks and the rest of the New Zealand Division massed behind the protection of Monte Trocchio. The two-company assault received the customary Nazi counter-attack, with some Panzers compelling a Maori withdrawal when their ammunition was exhausted while losing 125 killed or wounded. (*Philip Schwartzberg, Meridian Mapping, Minneapolis, MN*)

1944. Other elements of the 4th Indian Division continued the attack on the monastery on 17–18 February. However, with units of the German 1st Parachute Division situated behind minefields and barbed wire, the Indians lost almost 650 officers and men killed, wounded or missing. Across from the town of Cassino, two companies from the Maori 28th Battalion crossed the Rapido-soaked fields, using bridges and causeways that sappers had repaired under Nazi gunfire, and fought their way into the railway station on 17 February. Despite an extensive smokescreen to mask the engineers' work from German observers, crucial bridges to support Allied armour were not repaired, thereby limiting the attack to only a Maori battalion-sized infantry assault. The customary Nazi counter-attack with some Panzers ensued and the Maoris withdrew with their ammunition exhausted. The Second Battle for Cassino ended as the First Battle with the Germans in command of the town and, now, the ruins of the monastery atop Monte Cassino.

Third Battle for Cassino

The Third Battle of Cassino, Operation Dickens, occurred on 15–19 March 1944. Freyberg realised that it was vital to attack Cassino and the monastery from multiple directions and get both the tanks and the infantry assaulting simultaneously. He believed that assaults solely from Snakeshead Ridge and the various nearby hills west of Monte Cassino would fail. Thus, an Indian assault to capture the heights below the monastery was to occur in conjunction with the New Zealand assault on the town. With possession of the town of Cassino, the New Zealanders were to then dislodge the Germans along the heights by outflanking them in southward and westward movements to seize the railway station and, perhaps, a portion of Highway 6. The New Zealand advances were to facilitate the Indian units in reaching their elevated points to capture the monastery and perhaps seal the Nazi escape into the Liri Valley.

In Freyberg's final planning for Operation Dickens, Cassino was also to be assaulted by air during the morning of 15 March by 500 Allied heavy and medium bombers, followed by a creeping artillery barrage. Then the New Zealanders were to open their ground-attack at noon with A and B Companies of the 25th Battalion, 6th Infantry Brigade, 2nd New Zealand Division, moving through the northern part of the town along the Caruso Road, with B Squadron of the New Zealand 19th Armoured Brigade behind them, to the line of Highway 6 with the Hotel Continental as an initial target. Company D of this formation was to seize Castle Hill, Point 193, from their start-line (Point 175), and then be relieved by the 1/4th Essex of the 5th Indian Brigade, 4th Indian Division, prior to the latter unit's assault on its next objective, Point 165. Castle Hill was to serve as an advance point for other battalion-sized units from the 5th Indian Brigade, the 1/9th Gurkha Rifles and 1/6th Rajputana Rifles, to assault the hillsides above the town. Then, elements of the New Zealand 24th and 26th Battalions, 6th New Zealand Infantry Brigade, with Allied tanks, were to attack the town from the east and continue south with the railway station again one of the targets.

The Allied bombing and barrage of Cassino on the morning of 15 March levelled all buildings still intact, creating concrete piles and up to 60-foot craters that were impassable to tanks while providing the surviving Nazi defenders a host of ruins to become fortified defensive fire positions. Smoke and dust clouded the ruins as snipers killed runners and signallers to disrupt communications.

On 15 March, a platoon of Company D of the New Zealand 25th Battalion captured Point 165 only to take fire from Castle Hill (Point 193) on one side and from Point 236 above them. Two other platoons from Company D took the castle. However, the 5th Indian Brigade's 1/4th Essex did not reach the Castle until midnight of 15 March, several hours after the attack went in by the New Zealanders. It would not be until the early hours of 16 March that the 1/4th Essex reinforced Point 165. Companies A and B of the New Zealand 25th Battalion moved south towards the Hotel Continental, albeit receiving enemy sniper, machine-gun and *Nebelwerfer* fire from the town and nearby hills, which delayed their advance.

There was an insufficient amount of New Zealand infantry to press the attack as there was a delay in deploying the New Zealand 6th Brigade's 24th and 26th Battalions in their assault from the east. Even the German ground commanders at Cassino were perplexed by such massive firepower being employed, only to be followed by an infantry assault of a few battalions and tanks. Despite the tardy entry of the 24th and 26th New Zealand Battalions, by 17 March, the railway station was occupied by units from the latter battalion that had advanced southwards against a tenacious defence put in by elements of the Nazi 2nd Parachute Battalion. On 18 March, other units from the 25th New Zealand Battalion, which had kept moving south from Point 165, failed to capture the Hotel Continental. The railway station and other parts of Cassino were to remain in New Zealand-control, despite German counter-attacks.

On 16 March, almost twenty-four hours behind schedule, other elements of the 5th Indian Brigade went into action. Two companies of the 1/6th Rajputana Rifles attacked Point 236, but they were driven back to the castle, while two other companies from this battalion were lost to German *Nebelwerfer* fire and had not secured the intervening Points 236 and 202 to cover the 1/9th Gurkha Rifles attack on Hangman's Hill (Point 435). Nonetheless, platoon-sized elements of the 1/9th Gurkha Rifles ascended Hangman's Hill and made it to within 300 yards of the monastery's walls under the cover of darkness. However, they were to remain there in a precarious situation, reinforced by the continued gradual arrival of other small units from this battalion, receiving supplies only by airdrop or man-handling them up the height.

On 16 March, Kesselring transferred elements of the 4th Parachute Regiment to Cassino from nearby Colle Sant' Angelo, located to the west of Snakeshead Ridge

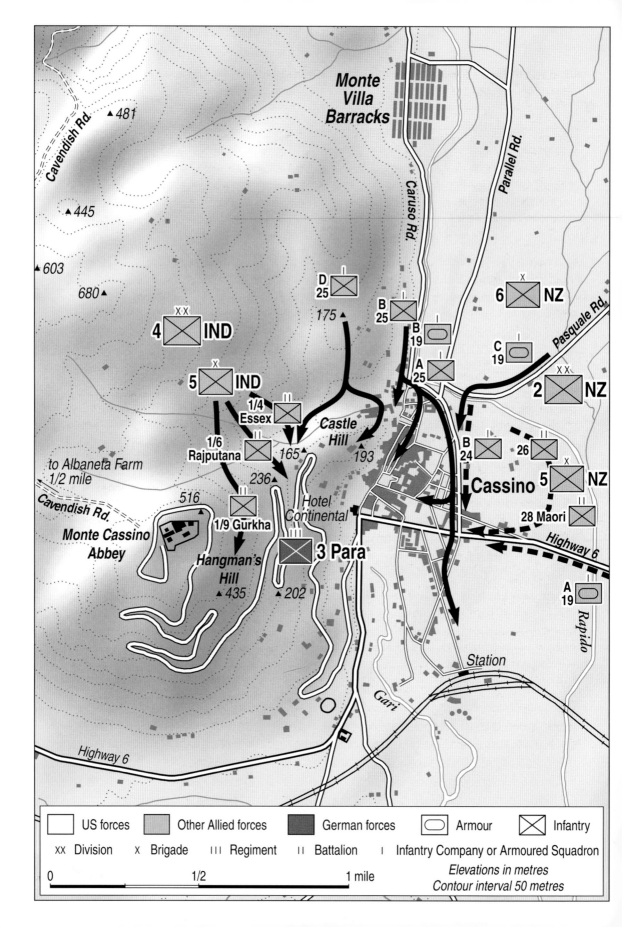

Monte Villa Barracks

Cavendish Rd.

▲ 481

▲ 445

▲ 603

680 ▲

Caruso Rd.

Parallel Rd.

D 25

175 ▲

B 25

B 19

6 NZ

4 IND

5 IND

A 25

C 19

Pasquale Rd.

2 NZ

1/4 Essex

1/6 Rajputana

Castle Hill

193 ▲

B 24

26

165 ▲

Cassino

5 NZ

236 ▲

516 ▲

Monte Cassino Abbey

to Albaneta Farm 1/2 mile

Cavendish Rd.

1/9 Gurkha

Hotel Continental

3 Para

28 Maori

Hangman's Hill

▲ 435

Highway 6

▲ 202

A 19

Rapido

Station

Gari

Highway 6

| US forces | | Other Allied forces | | German forces | | Armour | | Infantry |

xx Division   x Brigade   ııı Regiment   ıı Battalion   ı Infantry Company or Armoured Squadron

0   1/2   1 mile

Elevations in metres
Contour interval 50 metres

The Third Battle for Cassino. Following 15 March's massive Allied bombardment of Cassino, a platoon of Company D of the New Zealand 6th Brigade's 25th Battalion advanced from its start line, Point 175, to capture Point 165, only to receive enemy fire from two sites above them: Castle Hill (Point 193), and Point 236. Other D Company platoons soon took Castle Hill. However, the 5th Indian Brigade's 1/4th Essex reached Point 193 several hours later that day and only reinforced Point 165 during the early hours of 16 March. Companies A and B of the New Zealand 25th Battalion moved south along the Caruso Road towards the Hotel Continental, a Nazi strongpoint, accompanied by B Squadron of the 19th New Zealand Armoured Brigade. The advance was delayed by German fire from nearby hills and huge bomb craters. On 16 March, twenty-four hours behind schedule, other 5th Indian Brigade units advanced. Two companies of the 1/6th Rajputana Rifles attempted to attack Point 236, but they were driven back to Castle Hill, while another two companies were lost to German *Nebelwerfer* fire, failing to secure the intervening Points 236 and 202, which were to cover the 1/9th Gurkha Rifles attack on Hangman's Hill (Point 435). Nonetheless, platoons from the 1/9th Gurkha Rifles ascended Hangman's Hill on 17 March, making it to within 300 yards of the monastery's walls under the cover of darkness. Gradually, other small 1/9th Gurkha units reinforced them, bringing them to battalion strength. But their situation was precarious as ammunition had to be air-dropped or man-handled to them for the ensuing seven days. The New Zealand 6th Brigade's 24th and 26th Battalions' piecemeal attack, supported by armour, from the Pasquale Road was delayed, initially limiting the scope of the infantry assault to just elements of the 25th Battalion. However, by 17 March, the railway station was occupied by 26th Battalion units, which had advanced southwards through a Nazi 2nd Parachute Battalion gauntlet of fire. Hours after the station's capture late on the night of 17 March, New Zealand infantrymen had insinuated themselves on Point 202. From there, an assault on the Hotel Continental failed, with the attackers returning to their recently gained position along the hairpin turn adjacent to Hangman's Hill, staying there for the battle's duration. On 18 March, other 25th Battalion units from Point 165 also failed to capture the hotel strongpoint. The Nazis unsuccessfully counter-attacked Castle Hill on 18–19 March, but the German assault interfered with the 1/4th Essex reinforcement of the Gurkha battalion on Hangman's Hill. On 19 March, one arm of Freyberg's planned pincer attack on Monastery Hill failed when the 1/9th Gurkhas movement onto it from Hangman's Hill was stopped by German parachutists' small arms- and mortar-fire. The simultaneous assault on Monastery Hill from the west, along Cavendish Road, was launched with nineteen M4 medium and twenty-one M3 light tanks combined from the US 760th Tank Battalion, the 20th New Zealand Armoured Brigade and a 7th Indian Brigade Reconnaissance Squadron. The Allied armoured attack too was halted just south of the Albaneta Farm, as it lacked infantry support and experienced local commanders. Also, hastily sown Nazi landmines and German *panzerfaust*-armed infantry destroyed a score of tanks. The 28th Maori Battalion of the 5th New Zealand Brigade began its attack to capture the Hotel Continental and the Hotel des Roses at dawn on 19 March. However, it failed too. Freyberg's New Zealanders and Indians solidified their limited gains over the next four days within the ruins of the town, the station, Castle Hill and other small heights, amid sporadic local firefights. However, Alexander called off further II New Zealand Corps attacks on 23 March. During the night of 24 March, the Gurkha and Rajputana Rifles abandoned their blood-soaked positions on Hangman's Hill and the intervening territory between Points 236 and 202, respectively, both locales remaining as the German centres of resistance to the south-west of the town. (*Philip Schwartzberg, Meridian Mapping, Minneapolis, MN*)

and north of Highway 6. The weather also changed during the evening of 16 March, with rain beginning to fall. The next day, 17 March, saw the Third Battle for Cassino slide into one of stagnation, as terrain, debris and a yearning for low casualties forced both the Indians and New Zealanders to fight in small groups with limited armoured support. On 18–19 March, German parachutists attacked the 5th Indian Brigade's 1/4th Essex upon Castle Hill as they were deploying to reinforce their Gurkha comrades on Hangman's Hill. Ferocious close-quarter combat ensued with the Nazis eventually withdrawing.

A converging Allied attack on Monastery Hill was launched from two disparate locales on the morning of 19 March. From Hangman's Hill, elements of the 1/9th Gurkha Rifles comprised one salient of the assault. However, with persistent and determined German small arms and mortar fire from parachutists above them, and without adequate 4th Indian Division reinforcements, it was called off. A second, simultaneous assault on Monastery Hill from the west was launched with nineteen M4 medium and twenty-one M3 light tanks combined from the US 760th Tank Battalion, the 20th New Zealand Armoured Brigade and a 7th Indian Brigade Reconnaissance Squadron. This armoured movement advanced down Cavendish Road to the west of Snakeshead Ridge near the Albaneta Farm. The Germans were initially stunned by this bold thrust. However, the opportunity created by the Allied armoured attack was halted due to an absence of accompanying infantry to co-operate with the tanks, poor local Allied leadership, and Nazi minefields that were hastily sown but managed to destroy almost a score of Allied tanks to the south of Albaneta Farm.

By the end on 19 March, both New Zealanders and Nazis were still contesting for control of Cassino. The 28th Maori Battalion of the 5th New Zealand Brigade attacked from the east, but failed to capture the Hotel Continental or the Hotel des Roses. Four more days of limited but fierce combat at separate locales continued until Alexander called off further II New Zealand Corps attacks on 23 March.

Freyberg's troops solidified their limited gains within the ruins of the town of Cassino, while the Gurkha and Rajputana Rifles abandoned their blood-soaked positions on Hangman's Hill and the intervening territory between Points 236 and 202 without any further casualties on the night of 24 March. General Heidrich's parachutists' forward units had also been decimated out of proportion to the scope of the fighting as the Third Battle of Cassino continued to add to the German XIV Corps' losses by attrition in their defence of the disparate combat sites.

With a compelling need to craft a new attack scheme to reverse the three-month long string of failed Allied efforts to capture Monte Cassino as the strategic linchpin to breaking the Gustav Line, General Alexander began his operational planning for the May 1944 offensive, Operation Diadem, of which the Fourth Battle for Cassino would become a finale. The Fifth and Eighth Armies were to attack on 11 May under his unified command with a new strategic concept and his planned three-to-one numerical superiority in infantry.

Operation Diadem and the Fourth Battle for Cassino

On 1 January 1944, Lieutenant-General A.F. 'John' Harding, an experienced staff officer and desert field commander in Montgomery's Eighth Army, arrived in the MTO to become Alexander's chief-of-staff after recovering from wounds sustained while commanding 7th Armoured Division in North Africa. It was Harding who recognised that a major offensive on the Gustav Line along the Cassino–Garigliano Front was more likely to break the months-long deadlock than on the Adriatic one, so he recommended that Eighth Army's commanding general Leese re-deploy British XIII Corps west across the Central Apennines to occupy an area from the Liri River up to the south of Cassino on the eastern bank of the Rapido River.

Kirkman's XIII Corps comprising 8th Indian and British 4th Infantry Divisions in line for the attack, with the British 78th Infantry and 6th Armoured Divisions in reserve on the left flank of its zone south of Cassino. To the right of British XIII Corps was Anders' Polish II Corps' 3rd Carpathian Rifles and 5th Kresowa Divisions, along with the Polish 2nd Armoured Brigade in support, facing Monte Cassino and extending north opposite the Monte Cairo massif.

McCreery's British X Corps was transferred from the Garigliano sector to the northern Rapido zone in a desolate, virtually impassable mountainous wilderness area along the Central Apennines to become the right flank for the Polish II Corps. Freyberg's disbanded II New Zealand Corps divisions, which were taken out of the line for rest and re-fitting, would be situated within the new British X Corps sector along with a division-sized formation of Italian troops now fighting for the Allies. Allfrey's British V Corps remained on the Adriatic Sea coast.

Alexander shifted Clark's US Fifth Army, comprising the US II Corps and FEC, to the southern end of the Gustav Line. From the Tyrrhenian Sea, Keyes commanded II Corps' newly arrived 85th and 88th Infantry Divisions with the four FEC divisions (Algerian 3rd Infantry, Moroccan 4th Mountain and 2nd Infantry, and French 1st Motorised) on their right flank facing Castelforte, Montes Maio and Faito, as well as the Ausente River valley, which ran parallel to the Castelforte–Ausonia road. General Juin's corps would strike into the trackless mountains forming the southern wall of the Liri Valley.

Alexander and Harding wanted to wait until mid-May for the Allied offensive along the Cassino–Rapido–Garigliano sector, as drier weather and clearer skies would amplify the Allied advantages in armour and air power. Burns' I Canadian Corps, with its 5th Armoured Division and 1st Independent Canadian Armoured Brigade supporting the 1st Canadian Infantry Division, along with the 6th South African

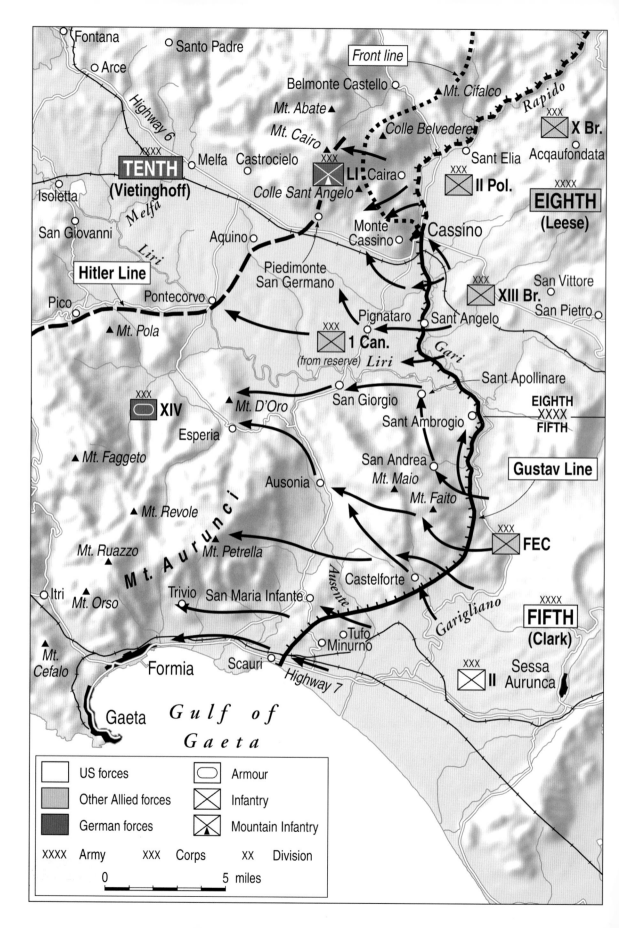

Fontana

Arce

Santo Padre

Belmonte Castello

Mt. Abate ▲

Mt. Cairo ▲

Melfa   Castrocielo

Colle Santo Angelo ▲

Front line

Mt. Cifalco ▲

Colle Belvedere ▲

Sant Elia

Acqaufondata

Rapido

XXXX
X Br.

Highway 6

XXXX
TENTH
(Vietinghoff)

Isoletta

San Giovanni

Melfa

Liri

Aquino

Cairo

XXX
LI

Mt. Cairo ▲

XXX
II Pol.

XXXX
EIGHTH
(Leese)

Monte
Cassino

Cassino

Piedimonte
San Germano

Hitler Line

Pontecorvo

Pico

▲ *Mt. Pola*

XXX
1 Can.
(from reserve)

Liri

San Vittore

XXX
XIII Br.

San Pietro

Pignataro   Sant Angelo

Gari

Sant Apollinare

XXX
XIV

▲ *Mt. D'Oro*

Esperia

San Giorgio

Sant Ambrogio

EIGHTH
XXXX
FIFTH

▲ *Mt. Faggeto*

Ausonia

San Andrea

Mt. Maio ▲

Mt. Faito ▲

Gustav Line

▲ *Mt. Revole*

Mt. Aurunci

Mt. Petrella

XXX
FEC

Mt. Ruazzo ▲

▲ *Mt. Orso*

Trivio

San Maria Infante

Castelforte

Ausente

Itri

Gangliano

XXXX
FIFTH
(Clark)

▲ *Mt.
Cefalo*

Formia

Scauri

Tufo

Minurno

Highway 7

Sessa
Aurunca

XXX
II

Gaeta

*Gulf of
Gaeta*

US forces		Armour
Other Allied forces	⊠	Infantry
German forces	⊠	Mountain Infantry

XXXX Army   XXX Corps   XX Division

0   5 miles

Armoured Division, were held in reserve to exploit a breakthrough into the Liri Valley.

Strategically, Operation Diadem was designed to engage German divisions that might be moved to meet the upcoming Allied invasion at Normandy. Also, it was Alexander and Harding's intent to destroy the German Tenth Army along the Gustav Line, not merely push it back to the next of Kesselring's defensive positions nor simply capture Rome. Unlike the Second and Third Battles for Cassino where companies and battalions were deployed, the two British generals planned to initially hurl two Allied corps, the British XIII and Polish II, against the Cassino fortifications, along the 7–8 miles of front extending from the foot of Monte Cassino to the Liri River, the locus of previous failed Rapido and Garigliano River assaults. Nevertheless, this attack route for Operation Diadem was selected as the only portion of the Gustav Line, against which Allied armour could be unleashed in strength of up to 2,000 tanks.

General Vietinghoff's German Tenth Army had to hold the sector extending from Monte Cassino south to the Liri River to prevent its bisection. Eighth Army's divisions were to be pitted against tenacious German parachutists amid the piles of stone rubble defences in Cassino and several *panzergrenadier* battalions dug-in along the

---

Operation Diadem and the Fourth Battle for Cassino. Seven weeks after Alexander's halt to the II New Zealand failed attacks during the Third Battle for Cassino, his broad, frontal attack utilising the bulk of four Allied Corps within the 15th Army Group was unleashed on 11 May 1944. At the southern end of the Gustav Line, the US II Corps' 85th and 88th Infantry Divisions attacked inland from the Gulf of Gaeta, from Tufo towards San Maria Infante and from south of Minturno along Highway 7 on the coast towards Formia. The American assault stalled, notably at San Maria Infante. The French Expeditionary Corps' (FEC) two infantry, one mountain and one motorised divisions broke the Gustav Line within twenty-four hours at multiple sites, amid difficult mountainous terrain. The FEC forces capitalised on their breakthrough and fanned out towards the foothills of the Aurunci Mountains, Ausonia, San Andrea, Sant Ambrogio and Sant Apollinaire by 13–14 May, sweeping behind the German lines towards the Liri Valley. By 15 May, the Germans withdrew from this area to avoid encirclement, which facilitated US II Corps' advance. Along the Rapido, XIII Corps' British 4th and Indian 8th Indian Divisions gained a small bridgehead across the river just south of Cassino and at Sant Angelo, respectively. However, sluggish reinforcement resulting from delayed construction of armour and truck-supporting temporary bridges limited a break-out into the Liri Valley. The British 78th Division added weight to the Rapido bridgehead on 14 May and advanced on Pignataro in the Liri Valley the next day, threatening an envelopment of Cassino's Nazi defenders. The I Canadian Corps now left its reserve positions and passed through the 8th Indian Division's lines, to advance through the Liri Valley. The Polish II Corps attacks on the Nazi 1st Parachute Division in the ruins and amid the heights above the town, constituted the Fourth Battle for Cassino, during which the Poles incurred steep casualties. On the night of 17 May, the Nazis withdrew from Cassino with the Allied moves into the Liri Valley, which threatened their escape. Atop Monte Cassino, the Poles hoisted their flag and trumpeted an anthem at noon on 18 May. Alexander broke through after nearly four months with *Diadem's* success triggering the break-out from Anzio, Operation *Buffalo*, to commence on 23 May, corresponding with the I Canadian Corps' attack on the Hitler Line at Pontecorvo. (*Philip Schwartzberg, Meridian Mapping, Minneapolis, MN*)

Gari and Rapido Rivers and beyond. Field fortifications had only been augmented after the three previous battles for the Cassino sector. The Allied Front was directly observed and covered by German artillerymen and mortarmen.

Frosinone and Valmontone to the north-west, both within the Liri Valley along Highway 6, were the main targets of Alexander and Harding after a strategic break-through at the Gustav Line. The British commanders believed that an Allied linkup of Truscott's VI Corps and the formations attacking through the Liri Valley at Valmontone had the potential of destroying the entire German Tenth Army. As future events were to unfold during the late May Allied offensives, both at the Gustav Line and out of the Anzio perimeter, Clark was not a believer in the British plans for a massive envelopment of the German Tenth Army. Clark's objective and target was to be for his Fifth Army to triumphantly enter Rome, the Eternal City.

The British XIII Corps was to batter the German defences and force a Rapido River crossing at Sant' Angelo under artillery bombardment. The Polish II Corps was assigned the capture of the heights of Monte Cassino and then move on to Piedi-monte San Germano, the northern anchor of the Hitler Line, several miles beyond the Gustav Line's defences. After breaching the Gustav Line, just to the south of Cassino, I Canadian Corps was to enter the Liri Valley and advance on to the Hitler Line defences with British XIII Corps on its right flank.

Regarding the German deployments against Operation Diadem, the XIV Corps' 94th, 71st, and a battle-exhausted 15th Panzer Grenadier Divisions, under Senger und Etterlin, was responsible from Terracina to the Liri River. The two divisions of the US II faced the German 94th Division's sector, while the FEC Corps, comprising four divisions including over 7,000 irregular mountain troops from the Maghreb, was to be pitted against the German 71st Division.

The *Wehrmacht's* LI Mountain Corps, under General Valentin Feuerstein, faced the British X, Polish II and British XIII Corps, and defended the northern half of the Liri Valley up to the southern escarpment between Monte Cassino and Piedimonte San Germano. This corps comprised the 44th Division on the southern bank of the Liri River; battalions of the 1st Parachute Division in the town of Cassino and within the monastery, the 5th Mountain Division, and elements of the 114th Jäger Division to the north of the parachutists. Group *Hauke*, a corps-sized formation formed by the 334th and 305th Infantry Divisions, formed the German Tenth Army's left flank extending to the Adriatic Sea coast guarding against British V Corps.

The British XIII Corps' attack by leading elements of its 8th Indian and 4th British Infantry Divisions at 2345hrs on 11 May 1944 initially appeared to be yet another failed Rapido River assault as the swift waterways' current capsized and swept assault boats downstream. However, other attacking battalions were able to make it across to form a limited bridgehead. Any advance was stalled by a lack of heavy weapons or armour support against a deep and continuous network of German field and concrete fortifications as well as minefields. Although the 8th Indian Division had two bridges spanning the Rapido River near Sant' Angelo by 0900hrs on 12 May, insufficient tank-bearing bridges were built by XIII Corps sappers, due to accurate Nazi artillery and gunfire driving them into cover. Kesselring, recognising that his Tenth Army's defences had been penetrated near Sant' Angelo, could feed in only piecemeal reinforcements to contest the British bridgehead. It was not until 0500hrs on 13 May that the British 4th Division was able to erect a bridge. On 14 May, Leese committed the British 78th Division from reserve to reinforce the 2,000-yard deep bridgehead amid vehicle congestion and muddy terrain. After three days of combat, Kirkman's XIII Corps was still unable to penetrate the Gustav Line south of Cassino into the Liri Valley, so Leese ordered I Canadian Corps to take over the front of the 8th Indian Division on 15 May.

The Polish II Corps' two infantry divisions struggled for two weeks before Diadem's start on the Monte Cassino–Monte Cairo massif. The rocky ground forced the Poles to burrow amid the protection of small stone sangars with any movement drawing German fire. The Polish assault battalions began their attack at 0100hrs on 12 May, incurring a casualty rate of twenty percent, but they were tardy seizing their objectives. Without proper reconnaissance, there had been no co-ordinated preliminary artillery bombardment of German positions. Nazi minefields prevented close Polish armour support with heavy casualties among the engineers trying to clear them. Finally, the Poles were pitted against the ferocity of the German parachutists. Within twelve hours of the start of the Polish II Corps assault, the tactical situation had become completely confused and the attack was temporarily postponed for reorganisation. Nonetheless, by 16 May, the Poles eliminated several Nazi defensive positions in a brutal struggle of attrition.

In the Tyrrhenian coastal area, the US II Corps attacks at the start of Operation Diadem on 11–12 May 1944 emanating from Tufo and Minturno failed. Near San Maria Infante, a battalion from the 339th Infantry Regiment, 85th Division, suffered over seventy-five percent casualties from German artillery bombardment and a stout Nazi 94th Infantry Division defence. The next three days saw little American progress, but suddenly on 15 May, the Germans began withdrawing due to the stunning FEC breakthrough of the Gustav Line from Castelforte to the Liri River and into the barren hilly terrain of the Aurunci Mountains.

The Nazi commanders deemed the FEC attack zone impassable, but elements of the 2nd Moroccan Division advanced 4 miles within twenty-four hours of Diadem's start, taking Monte Maio on 13 May. As German forces were intentionally thinnest in this mountainous terrain, FEC units broke through all along the sector. Elements of the French 1st Motorised Division arrived on high ground near Sant' Apollinare and were poised to move into the Liri Valley on 14 May. The Germans never recovered from this FEC breakthrough, with the *Wehrmacht's* 71st Division disintegrating after its flanks were enveloped, causing heavy casualties with 2,000 Nazis captured. The remnants of the 71st Division withdrew to the Hitler Line on 14 May, numbering only 100 combat-effective infantrymen by 18 May. As a result of the FEC success, the US 85th and 88th Divisions progressed 9 miles beyond the Garigliano River's mouth towards Formia against the hard-pressed German 94th Division. On 15 May, Kesselring agreed to a general Tyrrhenian coastal sector withdrawal.

On 17 May, Polish infantry battalions, under the cover of Allied fighter-bomber sorties, again failed to dislodge the Germans from Monte Cassino. However, the Nazi parachutists reluctantly abandoned their monastery defences on the night of 17 May as their escape route was threatened by advancing British XIII and FEC thrusts. The Poles renewed their assault on the monastery against German rear-guard units, enabling the 12th Podolski Lancers to hoist their standard over the ruined abbey on the morning of 18 May. British 4th Infantry Division units cleared Cassino, and sappers, including a South African engineer unit, began clearing Highway 6 of rubble for the movement of Allied armour.

US II Corps divisions took Gaeta and Itri on 19 May. FEC forces on that day crossed the Itri–Pico road, which connected Highways 6 and 7, and entered the Ausoni Mountain range. The next day, American infantrymen entered Fondi as the French continued their thrust towards Pico on the Hitler Line, the latter threatening to trap the German Tenth Army in the Liri Valley. A DUKW-mounted US amphibious from Gaeta captured Sperlonga unopposed on 21 May. Terracina, 10 miles further north towards the Pontine Marshes, was captured on 22 May, closing the gap to Truscott's VI Corps at Anzio.

Liri Valley campaign

The Liri Valley's terrain of thickets, vegetation and muddy ditches, provided excellent German defensive cover. Other than farm tracks, Highway 6 was the only major road. The Nazi defensive order of battle was the battle-depleted 1st Parachute and 90th Panzer Grenadier Divisions, with some tanks from the 26th Panzer Division. The strength of the German position in the Liri Valley was in its fortifications, especially the buried Panzer V (Panther) turrets, with their 75mm long-barrelled guns that were Allied tank killers.

After British XIII Corps' initial piercing of the Gustav Line, the I Canadian Corps received orders to advance on to the Hitler Line (also known as the Senger, Dora or Orange Line), several miles up the Liri Valley from the Rapido River. The I Canadian Corps made initial probing attacks on the Hitler Line defences on 19–20 May. The 1st Canadian Infantry Division launched its major attack against the Hitler Line, Operation Chesterfield, on the morning of 23 May at Pontecorvo, supported by Eighth Army's 700 guns. The Canadians broke the Nazi defences in a day's combat. However, the steep 'butcher's bill' amounted to 900 infantrymen and eighty Royal

Tank Regiment crewmen. A follow-up assault by British XIII Corps the next day broke this defensive belt completely despite counter-attacks by the German 26th Panzer and 305th Infantry Divisions. The Nazis soon retreated towards the *Caesar* Line, and the break-out from Anzio by Truscott's VI Corps, which was synchronised with the Canadian assault, commenced.

After Cassino, the Poles moved to clear Monte Cairo, which fell to reconnaissance regiments, the Carpathian and the 15th Poznan Lancers. On 25 May, Piedimonte San Germano fell to a combined-arms Polish attack, comprising the 18th Lwow and 5th Carpathian Rifle Battalions, the 12th Podolski Lancers, and the 6th Armoured Regiment. Total Polish casualties from 12–25 May numbered almost 300 officers and more than 3,500 other ranks, with over 800 deaths.

Also, on 25 May, Canadian motorised columns crossed the Melfa River further up the Liri Valley, while elements of the British 78th and 8th Indian Division took Aquino. On 31 May, the Canadians captured Frosinone on Highway 6.

North of Cassino, a US M4 medium tank from the 756th Tank Battalion is disabled off the roadside near the Rapido River on 8 February 1944. Elements of the US 133rd, 135th and 168th Infantry Regiments of Major-General Charles Ryder's 34th Division in US II Corps, accompanied by some tanks and infantrymen of 36th Division's 142nd Regiment (not used for the Rapido River assault), started their assault during the First Battle for Cassino on 24 January, and by 11 February almost succeeded in capturing the Benedictine abbey atop Monte Cassino. But the tenacious German defenders prevailed as the US II Corps attacks faltered. *(USAMHI)*

(**Above**) Castle Hill (Point 193) undergoing Allied artillery shelling, with the town of Cassino in the foreground, on 6 February 1944 during the First Battle for Cassino. At the time of this photograph, the Benedictine abbey upon Monte Cassino remained unscathed as per Allied headquarters' orders. The monastery had been built with 150 feet high walls that were 10 feet thick at their base. Left intact, it was to remain a dominating position with total observation to those inside over the Allied positions in the Cassino sector. (*USAMHI*)

(**Opposite**) An American B-17 heavy bomber just released its payload on the Benedictine abbey atop Monte Cassino as part of the Allied decision to unleash both aerial and artillery bombardment on the monastery on 15 February 1944. Approximately 250 heavy and medium Allied bombers destroyed the 6th century monastery. Ordered to unleash his 4th Indian Division against enemy positions leading to Monastery Hill on 15 February, and suspecting that Nazi observers occupied the abbey, Tuker requested the II New Zealand Corps commander Freyberg bombard the religious edifice. Successive Allied commanders Clark, Alexander and Wilson all agreed to Tuker's controversial request. Reportedly, German XIV Corps commander Senger und Etterlin sanctioned defensive positions to be situated near the monastery's outer walls with only the wounded allowed inside. (*USAMHI*)

(**Opposite, above**) A panoramic view of the Cassino battlefield from upon Monte Trocchio demonstrating the utter destruction wrought upon the Benedictine abbey and pertinent landmarks by the Allied aerial bombardment on 15 February 1944. The town of Cassino (*foreground*), the snow-capped Monte Cairo (*background*), Hangman's Hill (*far left*) and Snakeshead Ridge (*far right*) are all seen in this photograph. (*USAMHI*)

(**Above**) Two American artillerymen from the 36th Field Artillery Regiment pick up a 155mm shell to load into their M1 'Long Tom' cannon for their fire mission on the Benedictine abbey atop Monte Cassino on 15 February 1944. (*USAMHI*)

(**Opposite, below**) Near Monte Lungo, Battery D of the 36th Field Artillery Regiment fires its 155mm M1 'Long Tom' cannon from their weapon pit. Artillery positions such as these participated in the devastation of the Benedictine abbey, which transformed the fortress-like masonry walls of the monastery into fortified ruins for the German defenders. (*USAMHI*)

(**Opposite, above**) A ground-level view from the log-reinforced weapon pit of an American 105mm Howitzer during a firing mission on 15 February 1944. Smoke emanates from the abbey upon Monastery Hill in the distance. (*USAMHI*)

(**Opposite, below**) A New Zealand infantry section in house-to-house fighting in the vicinity of the railway station during the Second Battle for Cassino in mid-February 1944. The 2nd New Zealand Division had been brought over the Apennines on 30 January to relieve the Americans after their anticipated conquest. However, with the failure to capture Cassino by 11 February, the task for this second battle was assigned to Tuker's 4th Indian and the 2nd New Zealand Divisions now comprising II New Zealand Corps under Freyberg. (*NARA*)

(**Above**) Two New Zealand infantrymen move from house-to-house amid Cassino's ruined buildings during the second battle in mid-February 1944. The 28th Maori Battalion of the 2nd New Zealand Division, supported by other elements of the 5th New Zealand Brigade, attacked Cassino from the south-east during the late evening of 17 February, moving on the railway station and a collection of hillocks called the 'Hummocks', which were both close to Highway 6. Their aim was to construct, with the help of sappers, a route for Allied tanks to gain access into the Liri Valley. The Germans counter-attacked during the afternoon of 18 February, driving both the Maoris and sappers from the area of the railway station and Hummocks. (*NARA*)

A column of Gurkha infantrymen marches in single-file to the Cassino battlefield in early February 1944. These hardy soldiers in the Gurkha battalions of the 4th Indian Division (now part of the II New Zealand Corps) were from the mountains of Nepal and had an affinity for combat in such difficult terrain. The Allied commanders' strategy for the Second Battle of Cassino was for two separate attacks to begin on 15–17 February, with company- and battalion-sized elements of the 4th Indian Division's 7th Indian Brigade to advance southward from the previous US 34th and 36th Divisions' positions against elevated enemy points below the monastery. The other attack was to the town's east, and involved the 28th Maori Battalion seizure of the railway station and other locales in the vicinity of Highway 6 within the town of Cassino. (NARA)

(**Opposite, above**) An Indian muleteer of the 4th Indian Division leads his trio of pack animals through the ruins of the town of Cassino in mid-February to bring supplies to front-line troops assaulting the heights above. These sure-footed animals were vital as scarce roads were often blocked by rubble and vehicles frequently brought a rain of artillery shells. Freyberg opted for separate, non-supporting direct assaults against the town of Cassino and Monastery Hill, as he doubted that tactical and logistical support of his II New Zealand Corps' divisions could be adequately maintained by mule trains alone through the rugged mountainous terrain to the north and west of Cassino in mid-winter. (NARA)

(**Opposite, below**) The Allied bombing raid on the town of Cassino (*foreground*) and Castle Hill (*right background*) on 15 March 1944, prior to the attack by the II New Zealand Corps during the Third Battle for Cassino. Paradoxically, the devastating air-raid blocked Freyberg's armoured support as well as creating perfect defensive positions for German paratroopers who continued with their tenacious defence. (USAMHI)

(**Opposite, above**) German paratroopers setup their airborne variant of an 81mm mortar in a foxhole. The aerial and artillery bombardment of Monte Cassino created innumerable redoubts for such weapons that included shell craters, ruined building apertures and rubble piles. In addition to smoke and illumination shells, this mortar fired high-explosive rounds, which bounced back into the air before exploding. (*Author's Collection*)

(**Opposite, below**) Two New Zealand infantrymen cross open ground amid the rubble of the destroyed town during the Third Battle for Cassino, a series of II New Zealand Corps attacks and German parachutist counter-attacks at several locations from 15–19 March 1944. As is evident, mounds of rubble blocked all the routes through the town and limited movement of much-needed armoured support. Any attempts to clear the road debris by sappers were instantly met with accurate German mortar-, machine-gun-, tank- and artillery-fire. (*NARA*)

(**Above**) A New Zealand 6-pounder anti-tank gun crew fires a round from its weapon pit at German positions along the heights above the town in support of infantry from the 2nd New Zealand Division. Companies from the 25th Battalion, supported by tanks of the New Zealand 19th Armoured Brigade, moved south from the Monte Villa Barracks toward Cassino along Caruso Road that paralleled the Rapido River against fierce Nazi resistance. Castle Hill (Point 193) was captured late in the afternoon on 15 March by Company D from the 25th Battalion, but tardy 5th Indian Brigade reinforcement of this position enabled German parachutists from the 3rd Parachute Regiment to quickly strengthen the area between Castle Hill and the monastery in the waning hours of 15 March, preventing a rapid Allied seizure of the abbey from the east. (*NARA*)

(**Opposite, above**) New Zealand infantrymen are shown taking shelter behind a mound of masonry rubble and have the support of a New Zealand M4 medium tank in a British camouflage scheme (*right*). For the Third Battle for Cassino, Freyberg utilised infantry and armoured units to attack the town from the north and east. Companies from the 24th and 26th Battalions were sent in to follow up, albeit late, on the New Zealand's 25th Battalion seizure of Castle Hill on 15 March. (*Author's Collection*)

(**Opposite, below**) A New Zealand infantryman applies suppressive fire with his Bren light machine-gun at enemy positions situated beyond a smokescreen in the vicinity of Castle Hill during the Third Battle for Cassino that raged from 15–19 March 1944. New Zealand 25th Battalion infantry, supported by tanks, attacked through the rubble towards entrenched German machine-gun, mortar and artillery positions around the Hotel Continental and the Hotel des Roses, while other units from the 26th Battalion moving southwards captured the railway station. (*NARA*)

(**Above**) Indian infantrymen from the 5th Indian Brigade's 1/6th Rajputana Rifles cautiously advance through Cassino on 15–16 March 1944, during the Third Battle for Cassino, with an assortment of weapons including Short Magazine Lee-Enfield rifles, a Bren light machine-gun and a 0.45-inch calibre Thompson submachine-gun. (*NARA*)

(**Opposite, above**) German paratroopers defend their position amid the rubble with a light machine-gun. On 16 March, elements of the 5th Indian Brigade's 1/9th Gurkha Rifles established a position on Hangman's Hill (Point 435), 300 yards beneath the monastery's ruins. The Gurkhas remained isolated in that position for several days, exposed to Nazi parachutists' small arms-, machine-gun- and mortar-fire from above. (*Library of Congress*)

(**Opposite, below**) Polish troops slog through the mud on the move towards the Cassino sector of the Gustav Line as General Alexander brought as many divisions as possible from the Eighth Army's zone along the Adriatic Sea as well as newly arriving ones to Italy. The first units to arrive in the Cassino sector were the Polish II Corps, comprising the 3rd Carpathian Rifles Division and the 5th Kresowa Division, along with the Polish 2nd Armoured Brigade. (*NARA*)

(**Above**) Two Polish infantrymen from the 3rd Carpathian Rifles Division lob Mills bombs at German positions along Snakeshead Ridge, which ran to the north-west of Monte Cassino. The boulder-strewn ground that the Polish infantry was attacking, Point 593 at the southern end of the ridge, gave the German defenders excellent cover. This topographic feature had previously been unsuccessfully attacked by elements of the 4th Indian Division of II New Zealand Corps during the Second Battle for Cassino in mid-February 1944. During the Fourth Battle for Cassino, from 11–18 May, Polish infantry divisions were given the lethal task of capturing the abbey. (*Author's Collection*)

In the early hours of 18 May 1944, advancing Polish II Corps infantry units noted a German withdrawal from the ruined Benedictine abbey upon Monastery Hill. Polish soldiers from the 12th Podolian Cavalry ('Podole' Lancers) Regiment had cautiously raised their red-and-white insignia. At midday on the 18th, Master Corporal Emil Czech sounded the Polish St Mary's Trumpet Call (*Hejnat Mariacki*), a five-note, centuries-old anthem closely tied to the traditions of Krakow, to signal victory at the Fourth Battle of Cassino. (*NARA*)

(**Opposite, above**) Polish infantrymen conduct one of the few daylight reconnaissance missions to detect German camouflaged entrenchments in preparation for the Fourth Battle for Cassino, 11–18 May 1944. German parachutists in the ruined abbey atop Monte Cassino observed the Poles below, making their deployment extremely hazardous. (*NARA*)

(**Opposite, below**) Crewmen from two M4 medium tanks from the Polish II Corps' 2nd Armoured Brigade aid another of their 'Shermans' that had fallen off the roadway near Cassino during mid-May 1944. The presence of the Polish armour in the rear of Point 593, along with the supporting fire of the 5th Kresowa Division, enabled the 3rd Carpathian Rifles Division to capture this key position at the southern end of Snakeshead Ridge on 17 May. A counter-attack the same day on this locale by elements of the German 3rd Parachute Regiment failed to dislodge the Poles from their gain. (*USAMHI*)

(**Above**) The total devastation by aerial bombardment, tank- and artillery-gunfire is aptly demonstrated along the Gustav Line at Cassino. The town's ruins resemble a moonscape, with the heavily bombarded Castle Hill (*background*) serving as a grim epitaph to the success of the Fourth Battle for Cassino. (*NARA*)

(**Opposite**) A Fifth Army tank column, part of Major-General Keyes' reconstituted US II Corps, supporting the 88th Infantry Division, awaits orders near Tufo, on Highway 7, west of the Ausente River, to move out and start the attack against the southern end of the Gustav Line as part of Operation Diadem on 11 May 1944. As more battle-hardened Fifth Army American divisions shifted to the Anzio sector to bolster the perimeter and prepare for the break-out there, Keyes' US II Corps fielded two new divisions to the Italian theatre, the 88th and 85th Infantry Divisions. In this coastal area, the II Corps attack was initially indecisive for three days, until the Germans suddenly withdrew on 15 May from this most southern section of the Gustav Line. (*NARA*)

(**Opposite, above**) An American mortar squad moves on towards San Maria Infante, south-east of the Aurunci Mountains, in the US 88th Infantry Division as part of Operation Diadem on 11 May 1944. Detachments of the 88th Division went into the line at Cassino on 27 February, relieved the 36th Division near Monte Castello on 28 February, and replaced elements of the British X Corps near Minturno along the Garigliano River on 5 March. It was in this Tyrrhenian coastal sector that the 88th Division's 350th and 351st Infantry Regiments, as part of the truncated US II Corps, attacked the Gustav Line on 11 May and made little progress over three days against strong German resistance before an unanticipated German retreat on 15 May. (*NARA*)

(**Opposite, below**) American gunners of the 88th Infantry Division stand in front of their 57mm anti-tank gun and observe the ruins of San Maria Infante. On 12 May, the 351st Regiment of the 88th Division approached San Maria Infante and lost a company to tenacious Nazi resistance along the Tyrrhenian coast sector of the Gustav Line. In this coastal area, the II Corps attack was initially indecisive for three days, until the French Expeditionary Corps (FEC) penetrated the Gustav Line in its initial twenty-four hours of attack to the north of the Americans, hastening the Nazi withdrawal from the II Corps sector on 15 May. The Germans then offered only rear-guard resistance and the 88th continued its drive towards Itri. (*NARA*)

(**Above**) Infantrymen of the 88th Division, under German sniper-fire, race through the square in Itri past a German heavy artillery piece on 19 May 1944. Itri was situated on Highway 7 (Appian Way) at the extreme southern end of the Aurunci Mountains to the north-west of Gaeta and Formia. US II Corps' two divisions, the 88th and 85th, were moving towards Anzio to effect a Fifth Army link-up with Truscott's VI Corps, soon to break out of the perimeter there. (*NARA*)

(**Above**) Infantrymen from the US II Corps' 88th Division enter the ruined locale of Fondi on 21 May 1944. Fondi was situated in a triangle-shaped area inland from Terracina on the Tyrrhenian coast to the south-west, and Formia along the Gulf of Gaeta. Fondi was also located in the vicinity of the Hitler Line defences, which ran from Monte Cairo in the north along a south-western axis through Piedimonte San Germano–Aquino–Pontecorvo–Pico–Fondi–Terracina. On 25 May, a US VI Corps patrol met reconnaissance troops from US II Corps troops north of Terracina, four months after the original landings during Operation Shingle. (*USAMHI*)

(**Opposite**) American infantrymen of Company D, 338th Infantry Regiment, 85th Division, man their Browning M1917 0.30-inch calibre water-cooled machine-gun. These soldiers were firing on a German patrol in the in the US II Corps sector on 23 May 1944. In mid-April, most of the division moved into the Fifth Army sector of the Allied Front west of Minturno and faced the Gustav Line north of the Garigliano River for a month. On 11 May, the 338th Regiment cleared Cave d'Argilla, reaching Highway 7 at the road junction to Ausonia and Formia, just to the south-west of San Maria Infante, on 15 May. Formia was taken on 17–18 May. After an unopposed amphibious transport from Gaeta to Sperlonga on 21 May, elements of the regiment fought through a railroad tunnel and pushed on to Monte Leano on 23 May. (*NARA*)

An American mechanised column, supporting the 85th Infantry Division, moves through a war-torn street of Formia, situated to the north-east of Gaeta on 17 May 1944 after breaking through the Gustav Line. The US II Corps' two infantry divisions, the 85th and 88th, drove westward with the latter unit inland on an axis of Tufo–San Maria Infante–Itri. (NARA)

An M10 3-inch Gun Motor Carriage, named 'Clemenceau', of a French Expeditionary Corps (FEC) Tank Destroyer battalion, raises a cloud of dust as it crosses a restored section of previously demolished roadway in the Castelforte sector. There, Juin's FEC, comprising the Algerian 3rd Infantry, the Moroccan 4th Mountain and 2nd Infantry, and the French 1st Motorised Divisions, combated elements of the German 94th Panzer Grenadier and 71st Infantry Divisions during their offensive that started on 11–12 May 1944 and pierced the Gustav Line within two days, seizing first Castelforte and then Ausonia on 14 May. The FEC then drove along the north-eastern side of the Aurunci Mountains. *(USAMHI)*

(**Opposite, above**) An American soldier from the US II Corps' 85th Division mans his 0.30-inch calibre Browning water-cooled M1917 machine-gun with an Allied M10 3-inch Gun Motor Carriage tank destroyer in the background on 24 May 1944. The US soldiers and tankmen were covering two battalions of Nazi soldiers holed up in the Gallaeria di Monte Orso tunnel north-west of Formia. Troops from US II Corps were driving west to meet elements of the US VI Corps breaking out of the Anzio perimeter to the east of Latina and the Pontine Marshes. (*NARA*)

(**Opposite, below**) *Goumiers* of a Moroccan 2nd Infantry Division unit in the French Expeditionary Corps (FEC) load their British-issued 3-inch mortar for a fire mission against the German 71st Infantry Division in the Monte Maio–Monte Faito sector beyond the Gustav Line, which they broke through on 11–12 May 1944. The 2nd Moroccan Division mortarmen wear British Brodie-style steel helmets and their customary woollen striped coats, *djellaba*, typical of mountain tribesmen from the Maghreb. This mortar crew provided 'plunging fire' on the entrenched Nazi positions on the crests of mountains or heavily defended ridgelines. This FEC division made the 4-mile penetration of the Gustav Line in an area that the Germans believed impassable within the first twenty-four hours of the start of Operation *Diadem*, taking Monte Maio by the end of 13 May. This FEC advance precipitated the German withdrawal from this section of the Gustav Line two days later. (*NARA*)

(**Above**) A Moroccan *Goumier* mule train passes a French-crewed M8 75mm Howitzer Motor Carriage (*right*) and a truck carrying supplies to the front on 14 May 1944, near Ausonia, north-west of Castelforte, in the foothills of the Aurunci Mountains. The mixture of transports was emblematic of the fighting in Italy, where poor roads and mountain passes often precluded motorised attack and supply, the latter often left to the combat infantrymen with their mules carrying the munitions and rations. (*USAMHI*)

(**Above**) A British 25-pounder field artillery gun crew fires its ordnance as part of the artillery barrage that heralded the start of Operation Diadem on 11–12 May 1944. Hours later, the 8th Indian Division commenced its attack across the Rapido River which, after five days of stiff Nazi resistance, enabled a bridgehead to be secured to allow the British 78th Division to pass through at Sant'Angelo after the Indians had sustained heavy casualties. (*NARA*)

(**Opposite, above**) Infantrymen from the British 78th Division pass some of their entrenched countrymen along the side of the road just south of Cassino. On 17 May, these troops entered the Liri Valley and reached Highway 6 after their attacks crossing the Rapido River were delayed by tenacious German defence against the establishment of a bridgehead in Sant' Angelo. The eventual movement of the 78th Division into the Liri Valley north of Pignataro contributed greatly to the Nazi withdrawal from Cassino during the night of 17 May. (*NARA*)

(**Opposite, below**) Three British 78th Division infantrymen advance past a disabled German 75mm PaK 40 anti-tank gun after crossing the Rapido River bridgehead at Sant' Angelo and advancing to the north of Pignataro on 17 May 1944. The continued northward movement of the British 78th Division was intended to encircle Monte Cassino from the rear after crossing Highway 6, and threatened to sever the line of retreat of the survivors of the German 1st Parachute Division. (*NARA*)

(**Above**) Two infantrymen from the British 4th Division cautiously advance past a building in the south of Cassino under the cover of a Bren gunner (*foreground*) lying behind a disabled Allied M4 medium tank on 18 May 1944. The British 4th Division crossed the Rapido River to the south of the town days before as part of Operation Diadem. Castle Hill is seen looming high in the background. (*NARA*)

(**Opposite, above**) A British XIII Corps M4 medium tank emerges from a protective smokescreen in order to cross the Rapido River into the Liri Valley on 11 May 1944 as part of Operation Diadem. General Alexander sent two British XIII Corps divisions, the 4th British Infantry and the 8th Indian Infantry, across the Rapido River in assault boats on that day. German resistance to the assault was more intense than anticipated. Although both infantry formations had secured bridgeheads by the following morning, the assaulting troops on the far bank were amid Nazi pillboxes, barbed wire and minefields, which stymied their forward progress. The 8th Indian divisional sappers were able to erect two bridges across the river near Sant' Angelo by mid-morning of 12 May. Despite the gains, the bridgehead across the Rapido River was still shallow and heavily congested with many casualties incurred. It was not until 14 May that British 78th Division was able to cross at Sant' Angelo, pass through the 8th Indian Division and begin to move on to Monte Cassino's rear to the north of Pignataro in order to gain an entrance into the Liri Valley. (*NARA*)

(**Opposite, below**) At the start of Operation Diadem, at 2300hrs on 11 May, I Canadian Corps, comprising the 1st Canadian Infantry and the 5th Canadian Armoured Division, had been held in Eighth Army reserve. Here, a heavily camouflaged Canadian M4 medium tank from the 5th Canadian Armoured Division prepares itself to support British and Indian troops of British XIII Corps. The Canadians' mission was to pass through the British XIII Corps after the 8th Indian and 4th British Infantry Divisions crossed the Rapido and broke through the Nazi defences along the far banks of the river south of Cassino. Canadian armour and infantry were to exploit the access to the Liri Valley after British XIII Corps units cleared the town of Cassino and opened up Highway 6 towards toward the Hitler Line. The Canadians were to face elements of the 90th German Panzer Grenadier Division in their drive through the Liri Valley, which they had previously faced in both Sicily and at Ortona. (*NARA*)

(**Above**) Canadian sappers, as part of a I Canadian Corps motorised column, ready their equipment to dismantle Nazi demolitions left behind amid the ruins of Pontecorvo on the Hitler Line, which was attacked and pierced by the 1st Canadian Infantry Division on 23 May 1944. (*NARA*)

(**Opposite, above**) After being held in Eighth Army reserve for the pursuit up the Liri Valley and breaking through the Gustav Line in mid-May 1944, Canadian infantrymen and armour of the I Canadian Corps advance across a field towards Castrocielo, which was situated north of Aquino between the German Tenth Army's Hitler Line and the Melfa River, on 26 May. The tall grain that grew up during the spring months provided some natural cover for the attackers from the murderous Nazi fields of fire. The Canadians moved along a north-westward axis towards Frosinone located on Highway 6, with the British XIII Corps' divisions on their right. (*NARA*)

(**Opposite, below**) Elements of the 1st Canadian Infantry Division of I Canadian Corps cross the Melfa River over a sapling bridge on 29 May 1944. After piercing the *Hitler* Line, the Canadians came upon this water obstacle, 5 miles to the north-west. Under heavy Nazi mortar- and machine-gunfire, tanks of the 5th Canadian Armoured Division and Canadian Infantry crossed the river to forge a bridgehead. The 1st Canadian Infantry Division incurred several hundred casualties of all types, with the Germans defending the western bank being virtually annihilated. After the river barrier was pierced, the Germans withdrew to avoid being trapped in the Liri Valley. On 31 May, advancing past Ceprano, a crossroads on the Liri River, the Canadians, with British XIII Corps on their right flank, occupied Frosinone on Highway 6, concluding their Liri Valley campaign. (*NARA*)

(**Opposite**) Part of an Indian 8th Infantry Division section patrol the battle-scarred town of Pignataro on 18 May 1944. At the start of Operation Diadem, a week earlier, this Indian division forced a crossing of the Rapido River near Sant' Angelo. The Germans mounted a fierce resistance to the river assault and it took several days for the Indians to secure a bridgehead, through which the British 78th Infantry Division passed and headed north of Pignataro on to Monte Cassino from the west. (*NARA*)

(**Above**) Infantrymen from the 8th Indian Division of British XIII Corps advance with fixed bayonets amid the wreckage of Nazi planes and hangars under a protective smokescreen at an airfield at Aquino which, with the mountains in the background, served as an anchor for the Hitler Line. The airport was just east of the village of Aquino that stood behind the Hitler Line's wire. The Indian troops were to face elements of the 1st Parachute Division, which had withdrawn from the Gustav Line, and were arrayed along this section of the Hitler Line. Elements of British XIII Corps advanced south from Aquino to link up with the Canadians at Pontecorvo. The intent was that forces from the two Allied Corps would surround and destroy the German divisions defending the northern sector of the Hitler Line. (*NARA*)

An 8th Indian Division infantry patrol, led by a Bren gunner, wearing camouflage smocks, cautiously moves through Frosinone at the beginning of June 1944 looking for enemy stragglers. The town of Frosinone, a provincial capital on Highway 6, was a key road junction that linked the mountains with the Adriatic coast. Eighth Army planners hoped that the capture of Frosinone, by elements of the 2nd Canadian Infantry Brigade (CIB) on 31 May, would channel the retreating German divisions onto Highway 6 and subsidiary roads. Their strategic aim was for US Fifth Army to sever this major roadway to the north at Valmontone with the break-out from the Anzio perimeter, thereby trapping and eliminating enemy divisions before they could escape to Rome and beyond to fight again. (*NARA*)

Chapter Six

Breakout from Anzio and On to Rome

The US VI Corps at Anzio was gradually expanded to include three US (3rd, 34th and 45th) and two British (1st and 5th) infantry divisions; an amalgamation of the remaining rangers into the Canadian–American 1st SSF, the US 36th Combat Engineer Regiment, and the bulk of the US 1st Armoured Division. The VI Corps break-out from the perimeter was to start with Operation Diadem's success to gauge Kesselring's deployment of reserves. The re-fitted US 36th Division was sent to Truscott for his planned offensive, Operation Buffalo, once the Gustav Line was breached.

With the successful assault on the Hitler Line by I Canadian and British XIII Corps nearly complete, the VI Corps offensive was to commence at dawn on 23 May with the 1st Armoured Division-supported strike by the US 3rd Infantry Division at Cisterna first and then on to Cori and Valmontone, the latter on Highway 6. The US 34th and 45th Divisions were to advance on axes towards Velletri and Campoleone, respectively. On VI Corps' left, the British 1st and 5th Divisions' movements during the night of 22–23 May 1944 were feints preceded by an artillery barrage. Per Alexander, the Fifth and Eighth Armies along with VI Corps were to be pincers to destroy as much of the retreating German Tenth Army near Valmontone.

A tenacious Nazi Fourteenth Army's defence destroyed over 100 American tanks and produced nearly a thousand US 3rd Division casualties of all kinds. Over 1,500 Germans surrendered, yet the enemy still resisted at Cisterna the next day, despite Highway 7 being captured by the Americans, thereby severing the road link between the Nazi Fourteenth and Tenth Armies.

On 25 May 1944, the German 362nd Division was nearly destroyed by the US VI Corps at Cisterna. Also on that day, reconnaissance troops from the US II Corps advancing from Terracina across the southern edge of the Pontine Marshes linked-up with American engineers advancing southwards from Anzio. Truscott's VI Corps had re-joined Fifth Army four months after the Shingle landings.

Amid controversy, Clark diverted most of Truscott's VI Corps towards Rome up Highway 7 along the base of the Alban Hills towards the Italian capital on 26 May,

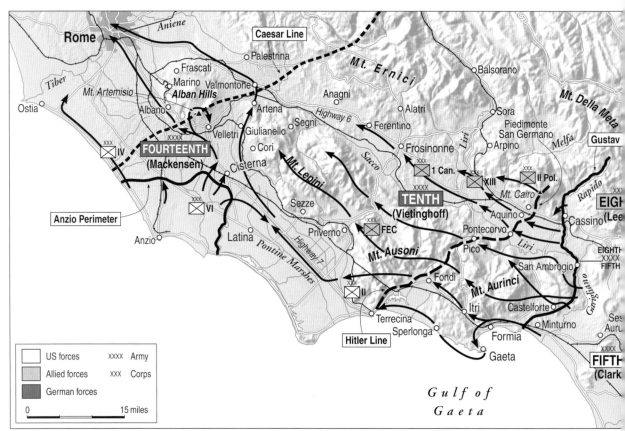

Advances to Rome. The US Fifth and British Eighth Armies' breakthrough along the Gustav Line from Cassino south to the Gulf of Gaeta (17–18 May 1944) coupled with the US VI Corps break-out from Anzio (23 May) produced an Allied two-front advance north-westward towards Rome. On 19 May, US II Corps troops advanced to Gaeta and Itri, while the FEC campaigned beyond Castelforte into first the Aurunci and then the Ausoni Mountains. After probing Nazi defences upon entering the Liri Valley, the I Canadian Corps attacked and broke through the Hitler Line at Pontecorvo (23 May) and then continued onto Frosinone (31 May) on Highway 6, with British XIII Corps on their right flank attacking Aquino. To their north, the Polish II Corps continued to advance through the Monte Cairo massif onto the northern anchor of the Hitler Line at Piedimonte San Germano. On 25 May, American engineers from Anzio met US II Corps reconnaissance patrols north-west of Terracina at the south-eastern end of the Pontine Marshes. On 25–27 May, Clark deviated from the Allied plans and shifted the VI Corps attack towards Rome along Highway 7 south of the Alban Hills against the German Fourteenth Army's defences along the Caesar Line, enabling the retreating German Tenth Army to regroup around Valmontone from the advancing British Eighth Army in the Liri Valley and the FEC campaigning in the Lepini Mountains. A new US IV Corps was deployed along the Tyrrhenian coast and advanced towards the Tiber River south-west of Rome. With increasing Nazi resistance at Valmontone, Clark re-oriented some of Truscott's VI Corps on an axis of Cisterna–Artena to comply with Alexander's strategy. On 30–31 May, US Fifth Army troops broke the Valmontone defences along the Caesar Line. On 3 June, Kesselring, with Berlin's approval, declared Rome an 'open city' with American patrols entering the Eternal City's outskirts on 4 June with sporadic rear-guard combat. Victorious American motorised and infantry columns coursed through the centre of Rome on 5 June, one day before the Normandy invasion was to unfold.

(*Philip Schwartzberg, Meridian Mapping, Minneapolis, MN*)

instead of moving north-east to Valmontone to cut off the German Tenth Army escape route in a pincer, with Eighth Army's movement up Highway 6 from Frosinone. Despite Truscott and other Allied officers' protests, Clark rationalised that the German Tenth Army was defeated and it was more militarily sound to get to Rome by the most direct route, Highway 7. Additionally, he wanted to avoid a German Fourteenth Army counter-attack from behind the Caesar Line defences in the Alban Hills on an exposed VI Corps left flank moving entirely on Valmontone. The normally diplomatic Alexander stated: 'I can only assume that the immediate lure of Rome for its publicity value persuaded Mark Clark to switch the direction of his advance.' Not willing to entirely ignore Alexander's directive to seize Valmontone, Clark sent a smaller part of VI Corps there to block Highway 6.

Truscott's north-west assault towards Albano was stopped by Mackensen's 715th Infantry Division in their Caesar Line fortifications. By 30 May, VI Corps' advance to Rome was stalled despite the insertion of the new US IV Corps into the advance along the coast from Anzio towards the Tiber River. For VI Corps to make a major leap forward towards Rome, a *coup de main* assault was unleashed by the US 36th Division, the Rapido River and Salerno veterans, up Monte Artemisio on the night of 30 May, which enveloped Velletri at the eastern base of the Alban Hills.

Also, Clark sent US II Corps on an axis from Highway 7 towards Artena and on to Valmontone, along with the FEC advance through the Lepini Mountains towards Cori and Segni. The retreating German Tenth Army was never entirely trapped by VI Corps' reduced force at Valmontone, as planned by Alexander.

Kesselring asked Hitler on 2 June 1944 to make Rome an 'open city', which occurred the next day, although he conducted rear-guard actions by elements of the German 4th Parachute Division to Rome's south and south-east, enabling many battered Fourteenth Army units to cross the Tiber River. On 4 June, a US 88th Division reconnaissance entered Rome with the 1st SSF securing five bridges over the Tiber. On 5 June, one day before the Normandy invasion, other elements of Clark's Fifth Army triumphantly entered the Eternal City without opposition.

General Harold Alexander (*left*), Allied 15th Army Group leader, and US VI Corps commander, Major-General Lucian Truscott, near battle-damaged Allied headquarters in Nettuno on 3 March 1944, discussing the continued build-up within the Anzio perimeter for a break-out (Operation Buffalo) to start on 23 May to temporally coincide with the success of Operation Diadem along Nazi Gustav Line. Truscott led the US 3rd Infantry Division and replaced Major-General John Lucas on 22 February as VI Corps commander. The 3rd Infantry Division was turned over to the aggressive Brigadier-General John 'Iron Mike' O'Daniel, the assistant division commander. Major-General Vyvyan Evelegh remained as Deputy VI Corps commander. (*USAMHI*)

Approximately fifty trucks, laden with large calibre artillery shells, wait aboard an Allied transport in Anzio Harbour. About twenty-five transports daily were off-loaded under the continuous threat of Nazi aerial and artillery bombardment, with a similar number of empty trucks taken back on the return journey to Naples. (NARA)

(**Above**) Remaining elements of the US 1st Armoured Division disembark from a Landing Ship Tank 77 in Anzio Harbour on 27 April 1944, as the break-out's build-up continued. With the German containment and indecisive counter-attacks ending on 20 February, combat was static and reminiscent of trench warfare during the First World War, except for the isolated attack, with frontlines often separated by less than 100 yards. (*USAMHI*)

(**Opposite, above**) British prime minister Winston Churchill complained about the extensive supply of the stalled VI Corps: 'This army is like a peacock … it is all tail.' As shown here, the 'tail' at Anzio was constantly supplied with amphibious DUKWs loading munitions and rations from transports offshore for the run-in to the beachhead's perimeter. (*USAMHI*)

(**Opposite, below**) British infantry reinforcements arrive at Anzio on 11 February 1944 to counter the German Fourteenth Army attacks that started a week earlier. The 168th Brigade from the British 50th Division replaced the decimated 3rd Infantry Brigade of the British 1st Infantry Division that had borne the brunt of the Nazi counter-attack at locales named The Thumb, The Factory and Carroceto Railway Station, during the first week of February. (*NARA*)

(**Above**) A British infantry section crosses a stream within the north-western sector of the Anzio perimeter near the Moletta River's mouth, probing enemy positions after the German counter-offensive ended on 20 February 1944 with staggering Nazi losses that forced the Mackensen's Fourteenth Army onto the defensive. (*NARA*)

(**Opposite, above**) Elite Canadian–American mountain combat infantrymen from Brigadier Robert Frederick's 1st Special Service Force attack a farmhouse during a raid near Ceretto Alto on 14 April 1944. Masonry farmhouses were fortified and transformed into entrenchments by the German Fourteenth Army now on the defensive. (*USAMHI*)

(**Opposite, below**) A British M4 medium tank lies disabled after hitting a *Tellermine* with a British Staghound armoured car (*left*) nearby. Limited counter-attacks were made in the western end of the beachhead by both sides in late February to early March 1944, with frontlines remaining virtually static after the massive German counter-attack concluded on 20 February 1944. (*USAMHI*)

(**Opposite, above**) German prisoners await evacuation to Naples on 17 March 1944. Earlier in the month, elements of the US 3rd Infantry Division regained Ponte Rotto on the Cisterna–Nettuno Road, with the assistance of tanks of the 1st Armoured Division, capturing many Germans. (*USAMHI*)

(**Opposite, below**) On 23 May 1944, Operation Buffalo, Anzio's break-out, commenced. Here, M4 medium tanks of the 1st Armoured Division along with motorised infantry from the 6th Armoured Infantry Regiment move forward along a muddy lane past their protective smokescreen (*background*). The primary target for Operation Buffalo was to pierce the German Fourteenth Army lines near Cisterna. (*NARA*)

(**Above**) The Italian town of Cisterna in ruins on 25 May 1944. Throughout the entire month of May, elements of the US 3rd Infantry and 1st Armoured Divisions campaigned near this locale as the main American point of attack during the break-out. (*USAMHI*)

(**Opposite, above**) American infantrymen take cover behind a Jeep along a road on their drive towards Cisterna in late May 1944. A German artillery shell had just detonated an American ammunition truck (*background*) that caused a huge explosion and smoke plume on the town's outskirts. (*NARA*)

(**Opposite, below**) A US 3rd Division rifleman fires at the enemy from a ruined building's window in Cisterna in late May 1944. Despite an extensive artillery barrage prior to the start of the Allied offensive, extensive German minefields took their toll on tanks of the 1st Armoured Division. Nonetheless, Cisterna was encircled and captured by the US 3rd Division on 25 May. (*NARA*)

(**Above**) A US 3rd Division infantryman walks amid the ruins of Cisterna on 25 May 1944. To the right, German corpses are sprawled along the street. The American thrust at Cisterna had decimated elements of both the German 715th and 362nd Infantry Divisions. (*NARA*)

(**Opposite, above**) American infantrymen search captured Germans in Cisterna on 25 May 1944. The quality of the recently raised German 362nd and 715th Infantry Divisions defending the eastern or Cisterna section of the Anzio perimeter was below the standards of other *Wehrmacht* Fourteenth Army divisions situated in the centre astride the Via Anziate; such as the Nazi 3rd Panzer Grenadier and 65th Infantry Divisions. (*USAMHI*)

(**Above**) An American soldier inspects a knocked-out German Mk VI (Tiger) tank in the town of Cori on 31 May 1944. After the capture of Cisterna on 25 May, elements of the US 1st Armoured Division moved quickly on to Cori, while others moved on to Velletri in the west. As planned, seizing the shoulders of the Velletri Gap would enable the bulk of US VI Corps to move north-eastwards to Artena just to the south of Valmontone on Highway 6. However, Clark veered his attack towards Rome. (*USAMHI*)

(**Opposite, below**) An American infantry patrol searches for Nazi rear-guard within Velletri's ruins, located to the Alban Hills' south-east, on 30 May 1944. The US 36th Division enveloped Velletri in a surprise nocturnal assault up Monte Artemisio the previous night. (*NARA*)

(**Above**) Two American officers peer into a German communication trench that led to a fortified artillery pit near Velletri. The gun's port faced the opposite direction (*background*), with the trench as the concealed means to re-supply and reinforce this weapon position. (*USAMHI*)

(**Opposite, above**) A British Jeep passes a German corpse on the roadside near the dead artilleryman's wrecked field-gun at Anzio perimeter's western end. After an initial feint, the British 1st Division attacked northward astride the Via Anziate, while the British 5th Division crossed the Moletta River and advanced on to Ardea inland from the Tyrrhenian coast. The German Fourteenth Army resisted the Allied advance from the centre of the bridgehead along the Via Anziate from behind its Caesar Line fortifications that blocked the southern approaches to Rome along the Alban Hills' lowlands astride Highway 7. Although Mackensen enabled the remnants of his Fourteenth Army to safely withdraw across the Tiber River on 2 June 1944, he was relieved by Kesselring on 4 June. (*NARA*)

(**Opposite, below**) A US 1st Armoured Division M4 medium tank, 'Weenie One', makes dust as it moves out from an assembly area towards the front-lines in the vicinity of the Velletri Gap in late May 1944. An *ad hoc* American armoured formation was tasked with interrupting the Nazi retreat along the road from Cori to Giulianello that commenced on 25 May. Hundreds of German vehicles were destroyed by American armour as well as by aerial pursuit. (*USAMHI*)

(**Opposite, above**) US II Corps infantrymen pass a road sign for Rome ahead and Frascati to the west as they advance north-west along Highway 6 north of Valmontone in pursuit of the retreating German Tenth Army towards the Eternal City in early June 1944. Days before, a US VI Corps engineer patrol linked-up with the 91st Reconnaissance Squadron from the 85th Division as the latter moved across the Pontine Marshes' southern end on the Tyrrhenian coast on 25 May to commence the re-united Fifth Army advance. (*NARA*)

(**Opposite, below**) One of the first American tanks to approach Rome is silhouetted by fiery remains of an enemy position near the city's railroad station on 5 June 1944. Limited Nazi rear-guard resistance was offered to the advancing Americans as Kesselring had declared Rome an 'open city'. (*USAMHI*)

(**Above**) The crew of an American 105mm M2 A1 Howitzer readies their weapon on Rome's outskirts on 5 June 1944. The gun's split trail mount is evident as the gunners shouldered some shells. (*NARA*)

(**Opposite, above**) An American M10 3-inch Gun Motor Carriage from a tank destroyer battalion fires on a German machine-gun position in the Roman suburbs on 4 June 1944. The day before, Kesselring declared Rome 'open', ordering his units to withdraw across the Tiber River. A Nazi rear-guard delayed the American entry into Rome, facilitating the German retreat northward. (USAMHI)

(**Above**) A US 1st Armoured Division column, led by an M10 3-inch Gun Motor Carriage, and a major-general's Jeep (foreground) await orders to cross a bridge into the centre of Rome on 5 June 1944. All the bridges entering Rome had been left intact by the withdrawing Germans. (NARA)

(**Opposite, below**) Infantrymen of the US 88th Division hurriedly pass a burning German Panzer Mk VI (Tiger) tank within Rome on 5 June 1944. Although battered like this German Panzer, Kesselring was able to take the intact remnants of his Tenth and Fourteenth Armies north to defend the Arno River and his newest fortification belt, the Gothic Line, which ran from Pisa to Rimini along spine the Apennine Mountains. (NARA)

(**Above**) Infantrymen of the US 85th Division pass through Rome's Porta Maggiore arch on 5 June 1944. A full-scale American movement into Rome occurred that day, while other American forces were deployed along the length of the Tiber River. (*USAMHI*)

(**Opposite, above**) An American M5 light tank passes over rubble in a section of Rome that had been bombarded by air and fired upon by advancing American artillery and armour. (*USAMHI*)

(**Opposite, below**) American Jeeps lead a US Fifth Army motorised column along a Roman boulevard with the city's inhabitants lining the sidewalks. As the evening of 5 June 1944 approached, King Victor Emmanuel abdicated his throne and placed his son as Regent. The Italian prime minister, Field-Marshal Badoglio, also resigned. (*NARA*)

In this iconic photograph, American infantrymen march around a portion of the Roman Coliseum for deployment to the north of the capital. Italian civilians look on impassively or walk by. *(NARA)*

Epilogue

The Italian mainland was invaded by Montgomery's Eighth Army on 3 September 1943 followed by Fifth Army's Salerno assault on 9 September. Italy had been knocked out of the war and a planned brief and limited Allied campaign evolved into nine gruesome months of horrific combat before Clark's Fifth Army's triumphant entrance into Rome on 5 June 1944 as the Allied prize.

Churchill was 'blinded by the prospect of seizing Rome and ousting the German forces from southern Italy by one magnificent stroke', with his advocacy for the Anzio assault. If the Anzio landings had incorporated a larger Allied force, Kesselring may have been confronted with the dilemma of abandoning the Gustav Line and retreating north to the Arno River and the *Gothic* Line. Likewise, the Allied commanders at Cassino utilised their strength inadequately when they wasted the II New Zealand and Polish II Corps divisions in limited, isolated attacks, in the least accessible areas, logistically and tactically, against a Nazi enemy holding the best defensive terrain of the fortified Gustav Line. With multiple Allied worldwide fronts and commitments, the resources allotted to the Italian campaign were not able to support more rapid, decisive campaigns to thoroughly overwhelm the Nazis, who repeatedly demonstrated their proclivity at mounting brutal counter-attacks to destabilise Fifth and Eighth Army strategic gains and tactical momentum.

Italy's geography and Kesselring's masterful defence to the south of Rome were other paramount factors that forced two highly mechanised Allied armies to advance at a delayed pace up the peninsula to the Eternal City amid battlefield gore over four months of stalemated combat at both Cassino and within the Anzio perimeter.

Upon examination of just the multinational Fifth Army losses at Cassino and at Anzio, there were almost 16,000 soldiers killed in action, with over 65,000 wounded and almost 14,000 missing in action. During May 1944's Operation Diadem alone, the *Wehrmacht's* Tenth and Fourteenth Armies suffered over 38,000 casualties, of whom 25,000 were killed, captured or missing. At Anzio, Kesselring estimated that during his February Anzio bridgehead counter-attacks and subsequent Allied break-out, there were around 40,000 German casualties, including 5,000 fatalities and 4,500 captured.

Yet Kesselring had managed again to extricate his Tenth and Fourteenth Armies intact and after withdrawing from the 'open city' of Rome, had a strong force to fight again north of the city. By the morning of 5 June, the Fifth Army possessed a 20-mile front along the Tiber and Aniene Rivers to Rome's south-west and north-east, respectively. The campaign beyond Rome had just begun.

(**Opposite, above**) The ruins of the Benedictine abbey atop Monte Cassino, with parts of the western wall and cellars still intact, viewed from Points 593 and 569. These hills to the west of the monastery were scenes of several failed Allied attempts from the latter half of January 1944 up until 18 May to seize the abbey in order to open Highway 6 into the Liri Valley. (*USAMHI*)

(**Opposite, below**) A dead *Wehrmacht* mortarman sprawls by his intact weapon after the final battle for the monastery on 17 May 1944. This Nazi soldier probably died of concussive injury from American artillery that had shelled the mortar position. (*USAMHI*)

(**Above**) Captured by New Zealand infantrymen and tankers during the Third Battle for Cassino in March 1944, the *élan* and hubris of German parachutists, wearing their characteristic knee-length camouflaged battle-smocks and round helmets, are shown. The four months of stalemated combat at Cassino was due to the tenacious Nazi defence amid the ruins and cratered battlefield. (*NARA*)

(**Opposite, above**) A British sergeant observes the relatively freshly interred German dead after Eighth Army's XIII Corps had driven on past Cassino to Esperia Montecelli, 25 miles to the south-east of Frosinone on 23 May 1944. German casualties during Operation Diadem were disproportionately enormous. North of Cassino, near Caira, was another graveyard that held almost 21,000 dead Germans from the southern Italian battlefields. (*NARA*)

(**Above**) Near Castelforte, a dead Tunisian of the French Expeditionary Corps (FEC) lies covered in a prone position with his shattered rifle besides him and his Adrian-style battle helmet upon his back on 13 May 1944. In piercing the Gustav Line at four separate places during Operation Diadem, the FEC had lost 2,150 killed and wounded, the Moroccan divisions suffering most heavily. (*USAMHI*)

(**Opposite, below**) The 93rd Evacuation Hospital at Anzio with one casualty about to be transported back to Naples. Many of the Allied wounded within the Anzio perimeter initially survived only to be bombed as they lay waiting for treatment or recovering from an operation. During February 1944, the American 33rd Field Hospital, the 56th Evacuation Hospital, the 3rd Division Clearing Station and the 62nd Medical Battalion were all attacked with both patients and nurses killed. (*USAMHI*)

Wounded Canadian soldiers of I Canadian Corps combating the Germans along the Hitler Line in the Liri Valley being led back to rear echelon aid stations on 23 May 1944. As cemetery headstones bear out, 138 Canadians from 2nd Canadian Infantry Brigade perished on this day trying to pierce the Hitler Line at Pontecorvo. (NARA)

At Nettuno, an American burial party commits a US serviceman to a final resting place during the battle for the perimeter. The Americans interred their Cassino dead, alongside those who fell at Anzio, in Nettuno. There were approximately 8,000 graves, and a memorial for almost 3,100 American servicemen missing. Just to the south of Highway 6 near Cassino, a British and Commonwealth cemetery held almost 4,300 graves with a similar memorial paying homage to the near 4,000 soldiers in the Fifth and Eighth Armies reported missing. (USAMHI)

References

Atkinson, R. (2007), *The Day of Battle: The War in Sicily and Italy, 1943–1944* (Holt Paperbacks, New York).

Black, R.W. (1992), *Rangers in World War II* (Ivy Books, New York).

Blumenson, M. (2001), *Anzio: The Gamble that Failed* (Cooper Square Press, New York).

Blumenson, M. (1970), *The Mediterranean Theater of Operations. Salerno to Cassino* (US Government Printing Office, Washington, DC).

Carver, M. (2002), *The Imperial War Museum Book of the War in Italy 1943–1945* (Pan Books, London).

Clark, L. (2006), *Anzio: Italy and the Battle for Rome – 1944* (Headline Review, London).

D'Este, C. (1991), *Fatal Decision: Anzio and the Battle for Rome* (Harper Collins, New York).

D'Este, C. (1990), *World War II in the Mediterranean 1942–1945* (Algonquin Books, Chapel Hill).

Diamond, J. (2017) *First Blood in North Africa: Operation Torch and the US Campaign in Africa in World War II* (Stackpole Books, Guilford).

Diamond, J. (2017) *The Invasion of Sicily 1943* (Pen & Sword, Barnsley).

Diamond, J. (2018) *The Invasion of the Italian Mainland: Salerno to the Gustav Line 1943–1944* (Pen & Sword, Barnsley).

Ellis, J. (1984), *Cassino: The Hollow Victory* (Aurum Press, London).

Fisher, E.F. Jr. (1993), *The Mediterranean Theater of Operations: Cassino to the Alps* (US Government Printing Office, Washington, DC).

Ford, K. (2004), *Cassino 1944: Breaking the Gustav Line* (Osprey Publishing, Oxford).

Graham, D. (1970), *Ballantine's Illustrated History of the Violent Century: Cassino* (Ballentine, New York).

Graham, D. and Bidwell, S. (1986), *Tug of War: The Battle for Italy: 1943–45* (St Martin's Press, New York).

Hapgood, D. and Richardson, D. (1984), *Monte Cassino: The True Story of the Most Controversial Battle of World War II* (Berkley Books, New York).

Hibbert, C. (1970), *Anzio: The Bid for Rome* (Ballentine, New York).

Majdalany, F. (1999), *Cassino: Portrait of a Battle* (Cassell, London).

Neillands, R. (2004), *Eighth Army: The Triumphant Desert Army That Held the Axis at Bay from North Africa to the Alps, 1939–45* (Overlook Press, Woodstock).

Perret, G. (1991), *There's A War to be Won: The United States Army in World War II* (Ballentine, New York).

Porch, D. (2004), *The Path to Victory: The Mediterranean Theater in World War II* (Farrar, Straus and Giroux, New York).

Tucker-Jones, A. (2013), *Armoured Warfare in the Italian Campaign 1943–1945* (Pen & Sword, Barnsley).

Werner, B. (2015), *Storming Monte La Difensa: The First Special Service Force at the Winter Line, Italy 1943* (Osprey Publishing, Oxford).

Whitlock, F. (1999), *The Rock of Anzio: From Sicily to Dachau* (Westview Press, Boulder).

Zaloga, S.J. (2005), *Anzio 1944: The Beleaguered Beachhead* (Osprey Publishing, Oxford, 2005).

Zuehlke, M. (2001), *The Liri Valley: Canada's Breakthrough to Rome* (Douglas & McIntyre, Vancouver).